'It is fair to say that psychotherapists and mental health professionals do not always show a capacity to translate their clinical knowledge into a language that can be understood by parents, carers and others involved with the care of children. But in this invaluable book, Nicole Vliegen and her colleagues manage to share the deep understanding they have developed, over many years, of children who have experienced early maltreatment and trauma, and give us an insight into how therapy can help to support them. The book is both realistic about the challenges these children and their families face, but also life-affirming. They describe the ways in which these children can be helped to evolve a self-narrative from "wounded and traumatised" to "scarred but liveable", and they do so in a language that will be accessible to all those adults who may accompany these children on their life-long journey'.

Nick Midgley, *Professor of Psychological Therapies with Children and Young People, Anna Freud Centre and UCL, London, UK*

'Tragically, this is a timely and much needed volume. With so much discord and unrest around the world, many children are experiencing prolonged and complex trauma. The authors have extensive experience working with children and families whose lives are coloured by trauma. They give readers a window on how trauma gets into the body and how their sophisticated, empathic approaches to treatment are impactful and lasting. Everyone working with vulnerable children will find this book invaluable'.

Linda Mayes, *Arnold Gesell Professor Child Psychiatry, Pediatrics, and Psychiatry, Yale Child Study Center, Yale School of Medicine, USA*

T0386341

Children Recovering from Complex Trauma

Children Recovering from Complex Trauma: From Wound to Scar draws on the latest knowledge and research on complex trauma in children, as well as the authors' expertise, in order to outline a trauma-sensitive approach to these children and their parents.

The first part of the book describes the emotional and relational dynamics underlying these children's behaviour. The second part of the book offers a glimpse behind the scenes of the authors' psychotherapy practice, elaborating the processes of change and growth that can enable developmental recovery 'from wound to scar' in children who have experienced complex trauma. As such, the book aims to 'demystify' what psychotherapy with a traumatised child may look like, as well as offer insights and tools which can support carers in their daily interactions with these children.

This book will be of great use to the adoptive parents and foster carers of children who have experienced complex trauma, and the care professionals (e.g., teachers, foster care workers) who work with them.

Nicole Vliegen is Full Professor in Clinical Psychology at KU Leuven, Belgium, where she heads the postgraduate training programmes in Psychodynamic Child Psychotherapy and Infant Mental Health. She is a licensed psychodynamic child psychotherapist, and heads the team of psychodynamic child psychotherapists at PraxisP, the clinical centre of KU Leuven.

Eileen Tang is a Postdoctoral Researcher in Clinical Psychology at KU Leuven, Belgium, and Assistant Professor in Psychology at Vrije Universiteit Brussel, Brussels, Belgium. She is a licensed psychodynamic child psychotherapist and is part of the team of psychodynamic child psychotherapists at PraxisP, the clinical centre of KU Leuven.

Patrick Meurs is Director of the Sigmund Freud Institute in Frankfurt, Germany, and Full Professor in Educational Sciences at the University of Kassel, Germany, where he is a staff member of the postgraduate training programmes in Psychodynamic Child Psychotherapy and Psychoanalytically informed Counselling for teachers. He is also Assistant Professor in Clinical Psychology at KU Leuven, Belgium, where he is a staff member of the postgraduate training programme in Psychodynamic Child Psychotherapy.

Children Recovering from Complex Trauma
From Wound to Scar

Nicole Vliegen, Eileen Tang and Patrick Meurs

Routledge
Taylor & Francis Group

LONDON AND NEW YORK

Cover image: Mark Borgions

First published 2023
by Routledge
4 Park Square, Milton Park, Abingdon, Oxon OX14 4RN

and by Routledge
605 Third Avenue, New York, NY 10158

Routledge is an imprint of the Taylor & Francis Group, an informa business

Original publication: Van kwetsuur naar litteken
© 2017, Pelckmans Uitgevers nv, Brasschaatsteenweg 308,
2920 Kalmthout, Belgium.

British Library Cataloguing-in-Publication Data
A catalogue record for this book is available from the British Library

ISBN: 978-0-367-72629-4 (hbk)
ISBN: 978-0-367-72628-7 (pbk)
ISBN: 978-1-003-15564-5 (ebk)

DOI: 10.4324/9781003155645

Typeset in Times New Roman
by codeMantra

Contents

Acknowledgements

First and foremost, our gratitude goes out to all the children who – sometimes more trustfully, at other times less so – dared to show us their vulnerable and hurt inner world, enabling us as therapists to walk alongside them on their journey at PraxisP, the practice centre of the Faculty of Psychology and Educational Sciences at KU Leuven, Belgium. In this book, we've named them Petra, Luke, Maya or Veronica. These are not the children's actual names, but the difficulties they face in life are certainly real. These children have taught us – through trial and error – to further refine our clinical and theoretical skills, resulting in the present book.

Of course, we are just as grateful to all the parents who contributed to this project: the parents who came to us for help, thereby affording us the opportunity to have a closer look together – sometimes through trial and error – at the often very vulnerable and painful themes they are confronted with as parents. There were also the parents who read parts of this book, who thought about it with us, who pointed out aspects that were lacking or that needed nuancing and who provided examples. It is for these children and their parents, and for others who are going through a similar life trajectory, that this book has been written.

We also wish to thank Christiana for sharing a part of her life story (pp. 15–16), in response to a newspaper article. Thank you to Kris Breesch, Anny Cooreman, Jos Corveleyn and Catherine Maes, who – as close colleagues and adoptive parents or foster carers – added valuable thoughts to the project. Thanks also to Erik De Belie for his constructive comments.

Moreover, our gratitude goes out to Stefanie Hesemans, who engaged herself in keeping us on track in this book project in several ways. She interviewed parents, and coached students in transcribing and processing of the interview data; she read and commented on the text; and she kept things together in an extremely meticulous and conscientious way. Likewise, Lieve Van Lier kept myriad book aspects together, ensuring this work was successfully brought to completion.

In addition, we are grateful to all our fellow psychologists-psychotherapists in the PraxisP psychodynamic team and of the Leuven Adoption Study (LAS). This work is, after all, the result of years of collaborating in and thinking together about increasingly better attunement of the mental health care we provide to vulnerable children and their parents: Eva Bervoets, Dries Bleys, Orfee Callebert, Sara Casalin, Ilse De Clippeleer, Simon Fiore, Karolien Hobin, Astrid Lauwereins, Saskia Malcorps, Let Moustie, Liesbet Nijssens, Femke Permentier, Hilde Seys, Lisa Vanbeckbergen, Ann Van de Vel, Camille Van Havere, Yannic Verhaest, Ann-Sofie Viaene and Sus Weytens. A special word of thanks goes out to Patrick Luyten as a close and ever-stimulating colleague, with whom we share a great interest in what makes child development and parenthood so special, and sometimes, also complicated.

We wish to acknowledge the colleagues at RINO Vlaanderen for their never-ending support for any new project, and the Pierre Vereecken Fund for the opportunities it affords us to continue to develop in an academic setting our insights into this important clinical theme.

We thank the colleagues at the Leuven Centre for Irish Studies, led by Hedwig Schwall, for the warm reception and hospitable place in which to write. We are grateful to Nancy Derboven (publisher Pelckmans Pro), who enthusiastically took on our plan when it was no more than a dream; to Hanna Maes (designer) and Mark Borgions (illustrator) for helping to make the dream come true.

We wish to express our appreciation to Libby Snape, for her support in copy-editing this English edition.

Finally, we thank Routledge publishing for their willingness to and support in publishing the book at hand.

The writing up of these acquired insights has made us richer people. As knowledge increases, wonder deepens, as Charles Morgan said.

**NICOLE VLIEGEN, EILEEN TANG AND PATRICK MEURS
JANUARY 2022**

Introduction to the English edition

> *Celine is now 13 years old. She's been with us for more than 10 years, so I'm starting to get some idea of what's going on inside her head, although I still have the feeling that I can more easily read my own (biological) children. (...) When we are having a row, none of my other children have ever said: 'I'm going to run away; you're not my mother! You can't tell me what to do. Why did you want me, anyway? You don't even like me, do you?'*
>
> CELINE'S MUM[1]

This book is written for the parents and carers of, and care professionals around, adopted and foster children who have experienced complex trauma,[2] such as those we meet in our daily psychotherapeutic practice. Mental health professionals frequently encounter these children in their work because they are so difficult to deal with. Their parents, teachers and other caregiving adults may often need specialist guidance to help these children grow towards adulthood without serious problems or lasting damage. Developmental tasks that are self-evident for other children, or which can be overcome with only minor hiccups along the way, are sometimes insurmountable obstacles for these traumatised children, bringing their development to a grinding halt. Such children are often labelled as having a developmental, conduct or attachment disorder – diagnoses that are not wholly unfounded, nor always unjustified. It is important, however, that a diagnosis is not used as the end point of a treatment trajectory, but rather as a starting point for further well-tailored treatment options that can reactivate the stalled developmental process. These children's difficulties are often the result of traumatic experiences in their early years of life. In changed circumstances or a new family environment, these early

DOI: 10.4324/9781003155645-1

experiences are not always recognised and/or accepted as still being relevant to the child's development in the here and now. These children and their parents deserve a 'trauma-informed' network (Osofsky, 2011), offering an understanding and evidence-based approach.

With this book, we wish to share with parents, carers and mental health professionals the existing knowledge about children who have experienced complex trauma, drawn from a variety of scientific sources and supplemented with clinical expertise. First, we wish to make the knowledge contained in the professional literature and text books more widely known, as a source of inspiration to find new avenues of approach to reach these children. References and sources of inspiration that have influenced our thinking and the way we work with such children and their networks are listed at the back of the book.[3] We describe how we have integrated these empirical and theory-based insights into our practice, and we offer thoughts and tools to interact with these children in a way that will optimise their developmental opportunities. Second, we wish to highlight the knowledge gleaned from our own empirical research conducted with adopted children and their families in recent years in the Leuven Adoption Study (LAS; www. leuvenseadoptiestudie.be), and in supplementary studies in which we interviewed children and their parents about various aspects of their social and emotional experiences. Third, we have been inspired by the clinical practice of PraxisP, the practice centre of the Faculty of Psychology and Educational Sciences at the University of Leuven. For us, PraxisP is a continually challenging natural laboratory that, thankfully, prevents us from becoming scientists in ivory towers.

At this point, it seems important to frame some of the local aspects regarding adoption and foster care policies in Flanders (the Dutch-speaking part of Belgium), which differ somewhat from those in English-speaking nations. In Flanders, adoption mainly concerns international adoption, in accordance with the 1993 Convention on Protection of Children and Co-operation in Respect of Intercountry Adoption. The group of domestically adopted children is very limited (about 5% of all adoptees), consisting of children given up shortly after birth following an unplanned and unwanted pregnancy, and only rarely as part of a child protection measure. Foster care placements happen in response to circumstances in which biological parents are unable to take care of their children, but unlike in other nations such as the UK, it is not common for children to be adopted from long-term foster care. Foster care only exceptionally moves on to adoption, for example, when the child has been orphaned. Foster care in Flanders comprises different measures, ranging from foster care in crisis situations to long-term foster care. Our day-to-day therapeutic practice – the experiences of which have formed the basis of this book – concerns children in long-term foster care as well as internationally adopted children.

Internationally adopted and foster children in long-term care in Flanders have a lot in common. Both groups of children grow up in families of caregivers who have chosen to raise a child that is not their own. As such, they have a history of at least one major discontinuity. Moreover, the fact that they have been in need of a foster or an adoptive family means they have often been through other early adverse experiences. This is why a subgroup of adopted as well as fostered children suffer from difficulties that can be summarised as constituting complex trauma. Undoubtedly, there are also differences: adopted children are their adoptive parents' legal children, whereas foster children will almost never be their foster carers' legal children. Most of the time, foster children still have a – legally recognised – bond with (one of) their biological parents; yet, especially in long-term foster care, the foster carers function as the child's substitute parents. They are often well-supported by the social worker of the foster care service, who also supports the biological parents. Therefore, the work with parents in our practice centre mainly involves work with adoptive parents, on the one hand, and foster carers, on the other. Hence, in the remainder of this book, for reasons of parsimony and readability, we will use the term 'parent' and 'caregiver' interchangeably when it is clear that it refers to the child's primary caregiver; that is, in the Flemish context, adoptive parents and (long-term) foster carers. When it is important to differentiate between biological parents, on the one hand, and adoptive parents or foster carers, on the other hand, or between adoptive parents and foster carers, we have attempted to do so.

Based on the knowledge regarding children who have experienced complex trauma, the main purpose of our book is to contribute to a societal basis for an understanding, trauma-sensitive approach to these children and their parents. We hope in this way to ease access to consultation and mental health care. Society's current emphasis on the need for 'good and competent' parenting sometimes increases parents' fear of seeking professional guidance, as was the case for Michelle, the mother of an adopted daughter with serious difficulties. It was only after several consultations that Michelle found the courage to tell her counsellor how she sometimes allows herself to react forcefully when feeling challenged by her adopted daughter's behaviour. It was clear she expected this information to be greeted with disapproval, whereas what she really deserves is understanding and support in her patient and never-ending quest to reach this 'difficult child'. We want to en-sure that the knowledge we have gained – both from counselling many children and from our conversations with carers, educators and other caregiving adults – can be placed at the disposal of the people who need it most: the children who are struggling through life, weighed down by the burden of past wounds, as well as the networks surroun-ding these children, who are trying their utmost to offer them every opportunity to develop optimally.

Writing a book on a complex theme of this kind is a bit like walking a tightrope. On the one hand, we want to share what we have learnt from these children and their families; on the other hand, we know that every parent – quite rightly – sees their child as unique, and not as fitting in this or that 'box', or needing a generic diagnostic label.

> *That sense of 'sameness' is something I have a problem with. It generates mixed feelings. In a way, it's good to know that Luke's behaviour is not so unusual, and that there are ways to handle it. At the same time, you want to keep seeing your kid as unique, and to not put generic 'labels' on him.*
>
> LUKE'S MUM

Moreover, it is most certainly not our intention to pigeonhole adopted and foster children uniformly under the heading of 'trau-matised'. For the well-adjusted children who are making their way through life with no serious developmental issues, this book will pro-bably offer little added value. However, the fact that their history con-tains at least one and sometimes multiple discontinuities in their early attachment relationships means that adopted and foster children are at greater risk of psychological injury of a traumatic nature than other children. This is also something we elaborate in this book. It is the group of traumatised adopted and foster children that most seriously confronts us with a challenging and sometimes arduous search pro-cess: a search for help that is appropriate, facilitates growth and offers maximum opportunities for optimal development.

It is also important to emphasise that this standpoint does not im-ply that adopted and foster children have a 'monopoly' on complex trauma. This book can also be relevant for children who grow up with (one of) their biological parents and are suffering traumatic psycho-logical injuries. That being said, the stories and examples in this book inevitably look at these problems from the perspective of adopted and foster children first and foremost, since these are the children who most frequently seek help in the practice centre where we work.

Within this context, we are very aware of the need to create space for unicity, because every child – no matter how seriously hurt – is above all, 'a child unique in their own being', as it was so poignantly expressed by Luke's mother. At the same time, we wish to give recognition to the comparable experiences that many children and their parents are faced with.

> *The fact that the stories of other parents are so similar really means a lot. It helps you to regain understanding, both for yourself and for your child. If other kids in other families are showing the same behaviour, you have to accept that something wider is going on.*
> MARIANNE'S MUM

This book consists of two parts. In the first part, we look at the way difficult experiences during the first phase of life can influence a child's development, and at the subsequent developmental problems this can sometimes create. We also seek to understand what this means for parents and for the child's network. In the second part, we give the reader a glimpse behind the scenes of our therapy practice, elaborating the processes of change and growth that can enable more constructive developmental pathways for traumatised children.

Notes

1 All the stories in this book are authentic and are based on the true-life histories of children and parents. To ensure anonymity and privacy, we have made these stories unrecognisable by changing details that are not essential to understand the context. All the names are fictitious.
2 In this book, we will refer consistently to 'complex trauma'; also known in the empirical and clinical literature as 'attachment trauma', 'early relational trauma' and 'early developmental trauma'.
3 The relevant knowledge and insights have been acquired from the many authors who are engaged in this theme worldwide. Subsequently, we have amended, integrated and applied this knowledge and these insights within our professional context. To make the book easy to read, we have avoided including too many references in the text. As a result, the list at the back of the book contains both referenced and non-referenced sources of inspiration.

Development: complex trauma

How difficult experiences early in life impact a young child and its carers

Introduction

In the first part of this book, we take a look at how difficult experiences in the early stages of life can influence a child's development. We also help shed light on what that means for parents and the broader network. In the first chapter, we describe the children this book is about, and the role psychotherapy can or cannot play in relation to the injuries they have suffered early in life.

Chapter 2 then explains what 'stress' can mean in the life of a very young child, and how chronic and heightened stress levels interfere with early development: having a traumatising effect on a young child's biological organism. To this end, we offer some insights from developmental psychology. A good understanding of what new parents are doing – without being constantly aware of it – to give their baby a good start in life helps us to understand what it means for a baby when 'good-enough' care is not present – even if only for a while.

In Chapter 3, we go a step further in understanding how children who have experienced complex trauma can struggle and get stuck with various issues and developmental tasks throughout their childhood and adulthood. We discuss how attachment and personality can develop 'atypically' or 'differently', and how this can continue to impact development long after these children's difficult start in life.

Finally, in Chapter 4, we discuss how parents and a broader caregiving network around a child who has experienced complex trauma can have an important remedial influence on their developmental trajectory. Nonetheless, this recovery sometimes requires a lot from parents, grandparents, teachers, educators and any other carers. We reflect on how this network can support a traumatised child's growth and development, rooted in an adequate understanding of the particularities of these children's functioning.

DOI: 10.4324/9781003155645–2

1 Special children, special care

DOI: 10.4324/9781003155645–3

Every child is different

> *Three-year-old Louise's adoptive parents consult for a diagnostic assessment. They are convinced she meets the criteria for an 'attachment disorder'. At home, they read everything they can on the internet about the disorder, looking for advice on what they can do to help Louise thrive. They are struck by a phrase used by one parent, who describes her son as 'a child whose needs are unending'. This captures the experience expressed by several carers, that whatever they do for an 'attachment disordered' child like Louise, it will never be enough.*
>
> *L[1] is eight years old. His behaviour is challenging at home; his adoptive father has already got to the point of taking the door of L's room off its hinges, because L sometimes goes into terrible rages against the door. L has also launched at his adoptive brother with a knife in his hand, when the brother grabbed his shoulders. 'We worry he will grow up to be one of those people who terrorise the Brussels subway' is the most frightening – but perhaps not unjustified – concern of his adoptive parents. They're at their wit's end.*
>
> *Maya, eight years old, can behave inexplicably badly in a way that exhausts her adoptive parents. In moments of blind rage, she kicks and bites, seemingly without cause. Her adoptive parents are extremely concerned about her development.*
>
> *Celine, 12 years old, throws tantrums whenever she has to get out of the car: she shouts and screams, and hurls the most awful accusations at her foster carers, without a second thought. She makes scenes that are seriously embarrassing for her extremely caring foster carers.*
>
> *Fourteen-year-old Veronica's carers consulted because their foster daughter doesn't speak for days on end at home. All she does is sit there staring angrily, ruining every family occasion. She can remain silent for hours and even days. When anyone else in the house tries to start a conversation, all they get is a snarl.*

On listening to parents' stories about their children, such as the ones described above, a broad range of issues becomes apparent. Often, these children exhibit severe behavioural problems, which can be highly disruptive for people around them. This is precisely why many of these children are initially referred for treatment because of a 'conduct disorder'. They appear to lack the regulation and control that many children of a similar age have already acquired; in some situations, regulation seems to be completely lacking. In many of these children, a minor – or perceived – trigger has major consequences.

However, there are also many situations in which these children seem to be able to remain in control of themselves and be perfectly well-behaved. It is precisely this discrepancy that doesn't always make things easier for their parents.

In a meeting between L's therapist and his adoptive parents and teachers, it is as though both parties are talking about a different child. In class, the teachers see a child who puts in every effort, even if this doesn't really result in any quick successes. The teachers look bewildered when the adoptive parents talk about L's extremely difficult behaviour at home. They can barely conceal the fact that they have serious doubts about these parents' parenting skills. In turn, the adoptive parents feel manipulated by their child: 'When he wants to, he can do it. If the teacher is standing next to him, he can grasp the course material, but if I do homework with him at home, it doesn't work'.

'If there is family around, she behaves herself, but as soon as she's alone with us again, she transforms into an uncontrollable monster'. Veronica, who remains silent at home for days on end, can appear to be incredibly social in other settings.

It is not always obvious that it requires enormous effort on the part of these children to behave themselves at school or on family visits. Back in the familiar home environment, they can let off steam and the parents' fears are confirmed: 'See, he's only ever like this with us'.

He had a very good tactic. At school, they never witnessed it, he worked very hard. When he came home, he was completely exhausted. He couldn't take any more stimuli, the phone had to be switched off. Then, when someone visited unexpectedly, he became hysterical.

LUKE'S MUM

> *At the parent-teacher meeting, Maité's sixth-grade elementary school teacher said that Maité would be able to 'manage general secondary education perfectly fine'. 'She's very diligent, very pleasant and polite, and I guess she is like that at home too'. I nearly fell off my chair. But I was glad she was doing well at school and her world was holding up. At home, she completely falls to pieces, because school requires so much of her energy.*
>
> MAITÉ'S MUM

It is these fluctuations that make it difficult to understand children who have experienced complex trauma. They come across as manipulative and consequently run the risk of being approached and treated as 'a manipulative child', which in turn reinforces their negative self-image. And the triggers are many.

> *L's adoptive parents describe him as manipulative because he lies: sometimes, when asked something, he pretends not to know the answer when he clearly does. He can be very sweet, so his uncles and aunts perceive him as a very pleasant child, while at other times – especially at home – he can make his adoptive parents' lives a misery. Moreover, he constantly feels hard done by: according to L, his brothers always have to do fewer chores in the house and yet, they get more clothes and presents. Whenever he gets something himself, he seems a little calmer, but his hunger for material things is so big that he is soon dissatisfied again; his frustration at what he is not getting is possibly even bigger.*

It is precisely this 'manipulative' aspect in these children's behaviour that sometimes makes parents wait a long time before consulting for professional help.

> *Veronica's parents talk about how she can sometimes convincingly 'play the victim role', making them anxious that a mental health professional would actually think they were not taking good care of her. At school, for example, she pretended that she wasn't given a dictionary at home and that's why she couldn't complete her homework properly.*

> *On passing a playground, L tells his teacher that he has never seen anything so fun. When the adoptive parents are subtly asked about this, they feel like they are being judged as neglectful parents, having never taken their child to a playground. They also feel betrayed by L: after all, they've taken him to a playground many times, so why would he say that?*

Although it is not always obvious, there is always a lot of anxiety concealed behind this difficult behaviour.

> *Louise and Maya keep having nightmares. Louise wakes up at night screaming and frightened; Maya has dreams in which her adoptive parents give her away.*

According to their parents, many of these children cannot handle losing in a game at all. However much these children love board games, they throw terrible tantrums when they lose. It makes one wonder whether in these children a minimal or unavoidable loss – like in 'Game of the Goose' – could perhaps be associated with a deeper, more existential sense of loss and lack.

To add to the confusion, these children are also more likely to exhibit unpredictable and difficult-to-understand profiles when it comes to academic performance.

> *Now, Maya seems to learn without any problems; then, she has unexpectedly poor results. L finds it impossible to master basic mathematics. His intelligence test indicates a mental impairment, but in other areas, he definitely doesn't always give the impression of having low intelligence. Veronica has severe dyslexia and dyscalculia. Celine advanced smoothly through elementary school, but gets completely stuck at secondary school level.*

Children requiring a manual

What these children have in common is their broad range of different developmental issues and the inconsistency in their functioning. These children seldom fit a profile that matches with one or other diagnosis. The multitude of issues often puts the clinician on the wrong footing in their assessment work, resulting in the children receiving a variety of diagnoses from different clinicians. Inconsistent, unpredictable and sometimes explosive functioning is what characterises them. As a result, they are assessed differently by one clinician than by another; or differently by the teacher than by the parents. However, it seldom occurs to people that such behaviour could be the consequence of the impact of a traumatic experience. Or, when trauma is acknowledged, it remains difficult to accept that it has an impact on all these behavioural, emotional or developmental problems, or even forms the connecting thread for them. People sometimes say: 'Okay, there's trauma in the past, but that can't explain the difficult behaviour in the here and now, can it?'

Precisely because of the significant fluctuations in their functioning, life with these children is sometimes quite difficult for parents. The parents sometimes express how they can't be an 'ordinary family'. What is fun for many children, such as going to the fair together or the prospect of a birthday party, is so overwhelming and exciting for these children that the fun dissipates in the tension and stress. Some children need solid rituals to be able to remain in balance.

For Maya, it is impossible to leave for school until all the crayons in her pencil case are sorted in the right way. Her adoptive mother invariably arrives at work late. Any attempt to get Maya to stop this ritual leads to scenes that only make the morning more difficult.

Tina mostly starts making scenes when it is time for bed. Her foster mother describes how the adrenaline is still flowing through her body for hours after the last flare-up, while she herself also needs a quiet evening and a good night's sleep to be able to start the next day with energy.

On top of that, in their search for balance with their child, the parents have learnt to manage some situations in a way that prevents things from escalating. They have learnt to choose their battles, and not to nitpick over everything.

> *Maya's adoptive dad doesn't get angry when Maya yells at him in the playground: 'Loser, is this what you call being on time?' He calmly says that he doesn't think that's how you talk to your dad, without going into further discussion or escalation. The fact that this is the best approach for Maya becomes obvious when – after behaving in this way for a long time – she sincerely apologises for her outburst in a later, similar flare-up.*

Nevertheless, this attitude on the part of parents is sometimes met with unsupportive comments. For example, they're told, 'I would never allow such behaviour', or 'If you allow all that, it's no wonder your child misbehaves'. The fact that behavioural and parenting difficulties can be linked to trauma, and that parents sometimes offer 'good solutions' to 'abnormal' behaviour, is not always understood by the outside world.

Being able and allowed to think about trauma in young children

It is sometimes claimed that babies or toddlers 'do not retain any trauma' of horrific events they witness; people simply assume 'the child is too young to remember'. Words to that effect were written in various newspapers in Flanders following a violent attack in a nursery in 2013. If only they were true! There may be a grain of truth in the statement, at least, when the circumstances following such an event allow for recovery – that is, when the children and parents in shock receive adequate support that enables them to give this trauma a place in their life story. When safe, competent and trusted caregiving figures are available, recovery progresses more smoothly and the consequences of trauma may be confined.

There are two reasons why we usually find it so difficult to dare think that even young children can be hurt psychologically and even traumatised. One has to do with how we like to perceive children; the other, with how we think about trauma. The first and perhaps most important reason is that we prefer to see, imagine and present our children in a healthy and flawless way. We see young children as intact and innocent. Knowing that good care is crucial for a young child's development, the thought that intrusive, shocking and traumatic experiences can occur at such a young age, and that the child can be seriously injured is almost unbearable. It takes a 'reset' in the mind of a healthy, caring adult to be able to imagine that many young children are exposed far too early to excessive stress – an event that can have lifelong consequences. Nevertheless, for children who have gone through painful experiences in their past, it is essential that adult carers are able to adapt their image of the innocent and intact child and be open to signs of injury. After all, these children need mental health professionals, teachers, doctors and above all parents (often including foster carers and adoptive parents) who pick up on their signals of injury and damaged development and who are willing to take the difficult path to support their child in building a life that is as balanced as possible.

This need is clearly not always recognised or acknowledged. Children who have experienced trauma in the past and grappled with it alone can sometimes look back later in life on their need for adequate help, and the fact that it was lacking.

I was two and a half years old when my mother didn't come back. She was injured in a bomb explosion on her way home and died nine days later in terrible pain from gangrene. It was 1940. My father stayed strong – 'crying makes you weak' and he wanted to set an example for his child. Women in my close circle did cry, but when I was around, they turned away or pretended they had a cold. Women in the street suddenly went silent when I passed by, or I heard them saying with pity, 'Luckily she's still too small to remember'.

My father never spoke about my mother, he had too much grief himself. He didn't realise that his silence evoked a lot of anger in me, especially when a 'new mother' unexpectedly took Mum's place. I couldn't express that immense anger as a child, and didn't dare to. The whole experience made me grow up as a tough woman.

Only when I was midway through my thirties did I start a process of recovery from the negative consequences of what had happened. It was a long road in which I was confronted with pain, sadness and anger for so many missed opportunities. It did give me the opportunity to ask for my father's forgiveness and to forgive him. By that time he was suffering from dementia and was crying all the time. Only I knew why. I am 75 years old now and only recently have I been able to give all the pieces of my life a place, to close the circle of my life story. The final piece was reading a book called Kind zonder moeder ('Motherless child'). The book helped me realise that my sense of loss was real, not imagination or self-pity. That's why I decided to write down my own story for myself.

*Life is good now. The absence that was always there, and that
I couldn't talk about with anyone, has now been compensated.
I am a happy woman, wife, mother of two daughters and wise
grandmother of a granddaughter and two grandsons. I'm glad that
children don't have to wait so long for help these days.*

CHRISTIANA

Trauma defined

As mentioned above, there is a second reason why, with children showing problem behaviour, we do not always immediately consider them
as processing difficult experiences. When we hear the word 'trauma',
we think first and foremost of a tsunami, for example, or a fire in which
the child lost their home; of a tragic car accident resulting in a great
loss of possibilities or caregiving figures, or a violent assault on the
street, and so on. Trauma refers to events that have a major and unexpected impact on daily life; experiences that are impossible to pre-
pare for. These are events that are so profound that our psychological
apparatus cannot process them in the way it can other experiences.
A person's life and psychological functioning is completely turned
upside down by trauma. We refer to type I trauma when someone is
confronted with a one-off incident (a car accident or tsunami). Type
II trauma involves recurring incidents, such as repeated sexual abuse
(by someone other than a primary caregiver). The third type of trauma
that is described in the literature is called 'complex trauma', but we do
not immediately think of it as 'trauma'. It involves a sequence of intrusive and/or discontinuous experiences within one's own caregiving
environment. It is precisely because of this latter aspect that complex
trauma differs from the other two types of trauma (see Table 1.1).

As adults, we can more or less imagine how a type I or type II traumatic event disrupts a person's life and functioning. What remains of
such a profound, harsh and overwhelming traumatic experience is a
'memory' of what happened. The experience is etched onto the memory like a stored film that contains all the details. In order to be processed, it is repeated over and over again and represented in dreams
and stories; the trauma has to be relived and told in order to give it a
place. The traumatic event needs to become part of or inscribed into a
person's life story, which is related throughout their life, written down,
and gradually rethought and rewritten. After a traumatic experience,

a person needs to be able to share that experience in order to give the event a 'place'. So, there is a great need for people who want to listen, and who don't get tired of listening over and over again; listening to a trauma story is often very upsetting. Likewise, there is a great need for people who also remain present when one can't or doesn't want to talk.

As adults, we can also more or less imagine that in processing a traumatic event, one can (re)connect to a significant extent to the strengths and resilient elements that have already been developed in psychological functioning. In difficult circumstances, some people like to tell their story to others; some are more likely to take care of others; still others react by working hard or playing sports, or they prefer to spend time alone. One person wants to share it, the other encapsulates it.

In children whose early development went relatively smoothly, a trauma with a significant impact not only disrupts their personal functioning, but often also compromises their overall development. Development that has progressed well up to that point is challenged to such an extent that there is an increased risk of developmental stagnation or mental illness. Various issues and symptoms may develop that can be considered as post-traumatic stress symptoms. Such symptoms

Table 1.1 Different types of trauma

	Type I trauma One-off incident	Type II trauma Recurrent incidents	Type III trauma Multiple incidents within the caregiving environment
Examples	A tsunami, a car accident, a major loss	Maltreatment, exploitation, sexual abuse (outside the caregiving environment)	Neglect, unpredictable parental care due to (mental) illness
Possible consequences	Overwhelming thoughts and feelings, excessive anxiety, nightmares, trauma triggers	Overwhelming thoughts and feelings, excessive anxiety, nightmares, trauma triggers	Fundamental disruptions in multiple developmental domains
Caregiving environment	Involved in trauma, loss of availability Existing care is source of resilience	Involved in trauma, loss of availability Existing care is source of resilience	Is (or has been) source of fear/threat/danger/stress Lack of 'safe haven'

can be found in many areas, affecting learning, social-emotional development and behaviour. They can also be very diverse: one child becomes very irritated and shows difficult behaviour; another child appears to adapt at first sight, but gradually becomes very withdrawn and inaccessible.

But what happens when the child has barely had any opportunity to lay the building blocks for constructive development and, moreover, is too young to be able to build up images or memories of (painful) experiences?

Complex trauma defined

So, in addition to the more clearly identifiable type I and type II traumas, there is a third type of traumatic experience: complex trauma, also referred to as 'early relational' or 'early developmental trauma' ('developmental trauma disorder'). It refers to traumatic experiences at a very young age and within the child's caregiving environment – the environment that should normally be a source of care and security and provide stability, but which for whatever reason becomes a source of fear, threat and danger; of lack of care, stimulation, warmth and love. Sometimes, it also involves unpredictable care, such as with the warm, caring parent who suddenly becomes aggressive under the influence of alcohol or drugs; or the parent with a psychological vulnerability who is sometimes unpredictable in their reactions.

Complex trauma refers to experiences such as neglect of fundamental physical needs for nutrition, warmth and nurturance, as well as of psychological needs for responsiveness, love, pleasure, stimulation and structure. It refers to exposure to direct or indirect violence, unreasonable or sadistic punishments, major unpredictability and/or experiences of loss. This type of trauma is often much less recognised as traumatic, yet it seriously affects a child's life and functioning, as well as that of the parents and other caregiving figures around the child.

Not only do such experiences become ingrained in anxieties and 'strange' incomprehensible feelings, thoughts or behaviour, but they also lead to the experience that life is unpredictable and unstable, that one can't rely on adults, and so on. Foster carers and adoptive parents often observe this as soon as a child who has experienced complex trauma starts to get attached to them after a while. Along with growing closer to each other, the injury or the rejection comes to life. It is just when parents spontaneously start expecting the relationship to deepen that the often bumpy journey begins in the foster or adoptive family. Therefore, children who have experienced complex trauma are sometimes labelled as having an attachment disorder: they do not have the most comfortable or consistent style for engaging in close relationships with caregivers, and they use these relationships in very different ways than other children (see Chapter 3). After all, it is precisely in relationships with their – biological – caregivers (attachment relationships) that these children have suffered injuries. These children have spent their earliest weeks, months and sometimes years of life in caregiving relationships where their needs and wishes were neglected, and where they were approached in an unpredictable or far too harsh a manner. Some authors (e.g., Jon Allen (2013) or Allan Schore (2009)) therefore prefer to refer to an 'attachment trauma'. The effects of such trauma become clear in various domains of development, and that is why other authors, such as Bessel van der Kolk et al. (2003, 2005, 2009), argue in favour of referring to it as 'developmental trauma'.

From wound to scar

At a very young age, experiencing is not yet about feeling and thinking. Rather, experiences are physically felt states and processes, the intensity of which is kept at a bearable level by the caregiving figure. Parents and other carers of young children prevent frustration, stress or excitement becoming too high, on the one hand; or will talk to, activate and stimulate a child who gets too far out of contact to interact, on the other. In traumatic situations of being ignored or neglected, or in situations of violence in the early caregiving environment, a child becomes chronically stressed above a bearable level, or learns early on that they are primarily dependent on themselves, as a result of which they become 'difficult to reach'. This process does not lead young children to have clear memories of what they are going through. Instead, the sequence of incidents leaves behind rather vague, physically palpable anxieties, or anxieties expressed in dreams and nightmares. There are no concrete reminders of what could be the cause or trigger of these 'strange' anxieties that the child is experiencing; there are no words for them either. In other words, complex trauma should be considered from the bridge that normally develops between body and mind (Schore, 2009). It appears to be the case that it is not so much the mind as the body of a child that carries the memories ('the body keeps the score', van der Kolk, 2014).

In this regard, we must not lose sight of the fact that this sequence of stressful and traumatic experiences takes place at a stage in a child's life when they are going through various new and crucially important developments. First, the child learns how to develop a basic sense of trust (first year of life); then they commit themselves to experimenting with their own autonomy (toddler phase); and then they are ready for the phase of healthy (sexual) curiosity (preschool phase). The child goes through all this during their first years of life, while also developing the ability to express themselves through play, words and stories. Inherent to complex trauma is the fact that all these domains inevitably become implicated in the traumatic nature of the event. When a caregiving figure, who is supposed to be the source of security and care, physically or psychologically injures or ignores or neglects a child, this results in the most fundamental experience of 'disruption' that we can imagine as human beings. Unlike other types of trauma, children who experience complex trauma do not have a primary caregiving figure who is outside the traumatising event and can take care of the traumatised child in a caring and non-traumatising way. In cases of complex trauma, it is the care itself that becomes connected with trauma from the inside, both in the child's bodily experience and in the otherwise barely representable psychological experience. From the perspective of an outsider, this experience is sometimes difficult to understand, but it nevertheless leaves a big mark on the architecture and the chemical processes of the brain and its associated stress system. This in turn impacts behaviour, (affective) experiencing, the way in which affects are regulated and later (caregiving) relationships are engaged in (Perry & Szalavitz, 2006).

Some children show a permanent hypersensitivity of the stress system or a permanent vulnerability in cognitive, emotional or relational development. Some children have been able to mitigate the overwhelming nature of this kind of trauma by becoming inaccessible or insensitive: they may have experienced the caregiving figure as having no interest in them at all, resulting in them experiencing an unbridgeable gap in relationships and never getting connected to their own psyche. Some children get stuck in the impossibility of distinguishing between what is caring and good for them, and what is a threat to them. These children sometimes lack an inner compass in this respect, as well as reject the compass that new caregiving figures try to offer them, thereby increasing the risk of repeating traumatic relationships.

In other words, traumatic experiences in the earliest months and years of life are formative for brain development and early personality development. They affect all possible domains of development, influencing learning, thinking and talking; they can colour emotions and relationships. For what other reason would some children continue to 'indulge' in extreme behaviour, even after years of living in a warm family environment with caring and reflective adoptive parents or foster carers? Why else would many new parental figures have to invest so much effort to achieve any feasible daily routine with the child? What makes some children pick up on so little of the positive care that surrounds them, and remain so focused on any lack? What makes some children develop persistent problems with reading and mathematics, and others have difficulty using language to achieve effective and nuanced communication about what is going on in their internal and external world?

Precisely because this type of traumatic experience takes place in a phase of life in which there is significant flexibility of development and many domains of development are still open, opportunities for growth remain. Processing within a therapeutic process can bring calmness and help things 'find their place'. Even when a therapeutic process does not lead to the 'recovery of all wounds', it can still be helpful for both children and parents to be aware of and manage these vulnerabilities more effectively, because it offers a unique opportunity to avoid getting stuck once again in later stages of development. With some children, living together in the (foster or adoptive) family will remain difficult or a source of conflict, but the difference can be that above and beyond these conflicts, a positive perspective can remain for the carers and the children. Through a psychotherapeutic process, the open wound or the encapsulated trauma can be approached and evolve into a scar, which replaces the original raw wound. Basic distrust can make way for viable relationships, in which (hyper)sensitivities can be taken into account. A scar is inherently less flexible than what could have originally developed in terms of relational flexibility in non-traumatic development. Yet, a scar affords more opportunities for a 'good life' than the open wound or encapsulated festering cyst of the raw trauma. A therapeutic process can thus fundamentally change the suffering, even if a scar will probably remain a sensitive or vulnerable spot for life.

Note

1 L was adopted from Africa and has had a very difficult life up until now. I (Nicole Vliegen) learned a lot from him and his adoptive parents. When I asked him if it was okay to write something about the therapeutic work with him, he explicitly asked me not to use a pseudonym, but to use his real name. It seems as though using his real name reinforces him in his identity and his story. In the end, we decided together not to use a fictitious name for him, but to use the first letter of his actual first name.

2 A little developmental psychology

DOI: 10.4324/9781003155645-4

A baby: a care-dependent and socially oriented being from birth

A baby is born with only a limited ability to regulate itself. For the first months and years of life, it is immensely dependent on caring others who see and understand what it needs. To compensate, the baby has a strong focus on those caring for it, and strong social skills that help it to relate to them. In the first weeks and months, the baby can smile invitingly, be movingly satisfied, cry when it needs someone and so on – all methods of keeping caring adults close by. So, from birth, communication with a baby is immediately two-way. Indeed, the baby recognises its parents' voice from before birth, their smell immediately after birth and their face only a few days later. It communicates long before it has any words at its disposal. For example, it expresses discomfort and fear through its facial expression, through body signals, movements, vocally and by crying. Both crying and looking away from what is causing the discomfort are socially very powerful signals for changing something in the environment. Conversely, laughing and making eye contact are highly rewarding ways of showing caregiving figures that they have got things right (Schmeets, 2011). Another channel available to the baby for arousal regulation is its motor skills. In difficult circumstances, for example, a child may become over- or underactive at a very young age (hyper- or hypoactivity), or its body may become too tense or too limp (hyper- or hypotonic). Eating and sleeping, too, can become part of the communication about how the child is feeling, from a very early phase (Derckx, 2011).

In other words, a baby is a (rather unique and initially nonverbal) social and active partner in interactions, who requires considerable attention, time and energy from parents and caregiving figures. The fact that a baby is continually dependent on these caregiving figures for various needs and expectations means that new parents often become good observers. They constantly look and listen to all the little signals and expressions their baby conveys through its body, face and voice for clues to how it is feeling and what it needs from them. It is one of the most important tasks of young parents to learn to 'read' their baby's body language and to give words to what they see, as well as to the motivations that lie behind it all (Derckx, 2011). Caregiving figures learn to find meaning in crying sounds, facial expressions, and ways of nestling, or not, into mum or dad. They learn to deduce from this physically expressed affective communication when their child is satisfied, hungry or in need of attention. In this way, a baby places its parents in a brand-new learning process that takes time and is largely mastered through trial and error, but for which both baby and parents have also been intuitively equipped throughout human evolution. Daily interactions, such as feeding and nappy-changing, are the perfect moments for a caregiving figure and baby to get to know each other. Looking at each other, touching each other and making sounds ensures a bond develops. In this way, the caregiving figure gets to know the baby's rhythm, as well as its needs and moods. In this early phase of the brand-new relationship, through the intense mutual exchange described above, foundations are laid for a lifelong bond.

A baby's cry has quite an invasive quality, making caregiving figures inclined to act quickly and adequately. Of course, it's no coincidence that such a cry is so penetrating. Evolution has made sure of it, and it is indeed essential for the developing baby that the parents react to it quickly and adequately. It is not by chance that care and comfort are so crucial for a human baby. Babies can experience primitive and raw feelings in the form of 'arousal'; unformed and still difficult-to-define negative emotions. These first forms of affect can overwhelm them and are difficult to deal with. All babies need an almost continuous presence and reassurance, but of course, there are also significant differences among them. Babies born prematurely or very temperamental babies require more from their young parents in this respect, compared to children who are born calm, or robust and mature. Some children's appeals are more intrusive; other children's are more difficult to respond to. Further on in this chapter, we explain what happens in circumstances where a baby does not receive an adequate response – for example, when there are no caregiving figures available during this early period of life, because they have died, are preoccupied with other worries or show no interest.

From shared regulation at the beginning of life to later self-regulation

The evolution from regulation processes managed primarily by the caregiving figure (co-regulation) to regulation by the child itself is an important first building block for the child's further emotional and relational development. As long as the baby does not have the physical and cognitive maturity to be able to wait for a bottle or a dry nappy, for example, it needs the caregiving figure to react quickly, precisely and subject to only minor cues. Initially, any moment of discomfort is primarily regulated by the caregiving figure: 'He will only fall asleep calmly if you wrap his blanket around him', or 'You have to hold the bottle like this, then she will drink more calmly and will have less cramping later on'. A feeling of security is created when the baby feels that it can count on being looked after, at its own rhythm and scale. Being reassured that your mum or dad is always there for you when you are in need; learning that when you are hungry, a filled belly will follow; that a caring figure always turns up when you feel alone in your bed; learning to enjoy cuddling and playing, being together and sharing. The baby learns it all during this initial time together. In the first few weeks, the baby relies entirely on its parents and surrounding caregiving figures to discover, understand and resolve its major and minor moments of unease and discomfort, as well as to help foster and share moments of positive feeling.

When the shared regulation is satisfactory and attuned to the baby's needs, it gradually gives way to increasing self-regulation. The body appears to store experiences of 'finding peace'. The child can then re-call these stored experiences more often. This happens, for example, when the baby can pull its blanket against its cheek, so that it feels exactly like when mum or dad tucks it in. During these moments, a child experiences – sometimes for the first time – that it can find peace and comfort and can evoke the 'mum-dad-care feeling'. What's more, the child can gradually start to endure a little delay as its body develops, and as its cognitive abilities allow it to remember that it can rely on caregiving figures. The baby no longer has to appeal to its parents by crying, but can occasionally regulate something by itself.

Processing information is building history

A baby's brain has been active since birth and it processes the continuous flow of information that enters via the senses (sight, sound, smell, taste and feeling). Information that is repetitive, safe and familiar forms an important initial memory trail. This is precisely why we make the world around young children as predictable as possible. When the baby hears the microwave 'ping', it knows its food is coming. Memory enables us to draw on past experiences to make the future predictable. A child gradually learns that mum or dad will always be back at their bedside when they show signs of discomfort or stress, they learn that food will always show up again when they show signs of hunger, and so on. As a result, the child no longer has to panic at every fear during the night or every feeling of hunger. In that respect, our brains are a historical organ; they store our personal history, even during the period when we do not yet have language at our disposal.

This means that all experiences leave their traces, including those that are painful or frightening. In a tsunami, for example, the child may have had the following complex of sensory experiences.

> *He first heard the panicked cries of adults, then saw and experienced how water flowed into the surroundings, heard loud sloshing and flowing sounds, then felt strange arms around his body, and heard strange loud voices. The combination of all these sensory experiences will create new connections in the brain. Later on, it may be enough that part of the network is activated (the sound of sloshing water), so that other aspects are automatically recalled (the image of water flowing in and the fear of that moment).*

The fact that the brain captures and stores all these experiences is a powerful trait that enables us to learn from experience. Through associations, we weave all incoming sensory stimuli into a whole. The fact that adults sometimes think that young children 'remember nothing' of early and very difficult painful events – and therefore do not (or cannot) suffer from them – has to do with what the word 'remember' means to an adult. The word 'memory' evokes how adults can recall certain events and express them in words. For example, perhaps you think of that warm summer evening in the south of France, how you sat there enjoying yourself when it suddenly started pouring down. Or you can think of that night when you were just sitting at home on the couch, when the phone rang and your father told you that your mother had died that evening. Or you can think of that wonderful party, and how nice it was that everyone made time to be there. What we store in memory, however, extends beyond what we can explicitly recall from events. There are also other kinds of memory traces, which are less comprehensible in language and can only be told to a limited extent, but which do play a role in the way early experiences get inscribed into our psyche. As an adult, you may have been able to experience for yourself how – after that telephone call when you found out about your mother's death – you suddenly started to tremble uncontrollably at every telephone sound. These memory traces bypass conscious, conceptual functioning. They are memory traces of a different quality; they nestle in the psyche of a young child and can influence their further development and behaviour, without the child having any conscious awareness of it.

What if we didn't reassure and comfort?

An experiment conducted by Edward Tronick in 1975 provided crucial insights into how a lack of affective responsiveness in the caregiving figure leads to intense stress in young children. He simulated a mini situation in a laboratory in which a caregiving figure is physically present for a short period of time (three minutes), but emotionally unavailable to the child. The experiment was called the 'still face' experiment (https://youtu.be/apzXGEbZht0) and moves through four phases:

1 A baby is placed in a chair opposite his mother so they can easily look at each other. The mother is asked to simply interact with her child in the way she usually does.
2 This is followed by a three-minute episode in which the mother keeps her facial expression completely blank. What happens during these three minutes shows the young child's huge need for social interaction. In the first instance, the child reacts with various initiatives to try to restore the familiar interaction. The baby smiles at his mother, hoping she will smile back, as he is used to her responding to his invitation to interact. He extends his little arms to her, expecting her to pick him up. He points his little finger to a place behind her, assuming she will turn to look.
3 The extent to which the child finds the mother's lack of response distressing is reflected in what happens next. Gradually realising that she is not reacting at all, the baby shows through his behaviour negative feelings that become more and more intense, and which gradually turn into panic. The child is genuinely distraught. There are also somatic signs of severe discomfort and stress in the baby. For example, his increased heart rate indicates that the child is experiencing significant stress. In some babies, the stress becomes so intense they start gagging.
4 When, after three agonising minutes, the mother is given a sign that she can connect to the baby again, the baby's heartbeat slows down and he then experiences different feelings – for example, comfort following the sadness endured, or joy at finding Mummy again.

Importance of repair in interactions

What is described above is what happens to children who are used to 'responsive social contact'. These children have learnt that caregiving figures smile at them, talk (or make baby noises) with them and look together at what they find interesting. These children also experience intense pleasure in such exchanges. However, more recent research by Haley and Stansbury (2003) shows what happens to babies who grow up in an environment characterised by a constant lack of responsiveness. These babies have primarily experienced and learnt how reactions and relationships are unpredictable in terms of responsiveness.

These children also react to the loss of interaction with negative feelings and physical stress complaints, such as an increased heart rate –
in this respect, they are no different from the children who are used
to responsive caregiving figures. However, what is striking is what
happens after the 'still face' episode. The negative feelings and increased heart rate persist much longer, despite the mother's resumed
responsiveness. This means that the more children are exposed to less
responsive interactions, the more stress they experience in those interactions. Also, the harder it is and longer it takes for the positive affects
or the milder reactions to re-emerge.

Positive interactive moments are described as moments when there
is a 'match' – attunement or connectedness – between the child and its
caregiving figure. It is a human trait to have a strong longing for these
moments of 'positive matching'. But the negative moments in which
frustration, sadness, being left alone or misunderstanding predomi-
nate, are also part and parcel of any child's life. Think of moments
when a caregiving figure does not have much time in the morning, or
moments when a caregiving figure is preoccupied with other concerns.
These moments of 'mismatch' in no way endanger a child's development. They are, on the contrary, an essential part of growing up. It is
precisely at these moments that a child learns a lot about themselves
and about life. A baby, for example, learns that it may have to wait
a while or to feel that it's not such a terrible thing that mum doesn't
have time for it right now, but that she will be there for it again soon.
It sharpens the child's vigilance and their powers of observation when
they notice that dad organises the bedtime ritual differently from how
mum does it. Nonetheless, the essential aspect is the idea of 'repair' in
interactions: a moment of mismatch or 'losing each other' is followed
by 'finding each other again'; a mismatch is repaired and followed by
a moment of matching.

---

*Edward Tronick observed parent-child interactions among 'nor-
mal' parents who interacted with their child in a way that was good
enough. He found that only 30% of the time, during quiet moments
of play, a state of understanding or match could be observed. He
concluded from these and other studies that the ability of caregiving figures to repair moments of mismatch is fundamental to good
(attachment) development.*

What is taxing and traumatising for children are the moments of negativity and overwhelming affect that become permanent, that do not get repaired. Crying incessantly and never being reassured that someone will show up; a feeling of hunger that leads to overwhelming panic over and over again; no one ever noticing that the child could use some motor or cognitive stimulation; caregiving figures who, due to circumstances such as serious illness or grief, only focus on themselves and their own equilibrium, or who are psychologically ill, meaning that they rarely notice what the child is trying to show them. When the early stages of life are characterised – for whatever reason – by a lack of care or by very unpredictable care, the normal developmental tasks and stages that children seem to learn by themselves in good-enough circumstances remain highly sensitive or vulnerable for a very long time, or even for life. Then, learning to deal with waiting and lack, with what one is not allowed or does not receive, often triggers those overwhelming old feelings of having had to wait too early in life, too much and too long for food, stimulation or care. Again and again, the old feelings of fundamental lack are stuck onto new experiences.

> *Following Tronick and Gianino's (1986) groundbreaking work, research has amply shown that a sequence of match, mismatch and repair forms the basis of any relationship that is 'good enough'. Lack of repair is the striking line between a context that is 'good enough' versus a context that is a source of traumatic experience.*

For children who grew up in such circumstances, a 'normal' parental limit set by new and/or caring caregiving figures (foster carer or adoptive parent or teacher) can evoke intense feelings of 'not being loved', 'being allowed to do less, and receiving less, than brother or sister', etc., for a long time. Losing in a board game can continue to evoke a deep and fundamental loss, over and over again, making it so much more difficult to bear. Every feeling of hunger – no matter how small – can lead to a feeling of complete deprivation, or to the associated emotional overwhelm by negative affect, lack of regulation or even complete withdrawal from the relationship with the caregiving figure. This means parents are confronted with what they feel is an 'exaggerated' reaction to a mundane incident: they see the child going into a violent rage or being standoffish, whereas in their eyes, nothing justifies such an intense reaction.

Complex trauma: a backpack filled with overwhelming experiences

Optimal development requires an appropriate regulating approach from the parent that is attuned to the baby's or young child's early regulating capabilities. For this, there needs to be a caring context and social support around the child and their caregiving figures (Osofsky, 2011). In this regard, Gunnar and Quevedo (2007) stated 'Caregivers and close relatives in a child's life are both potentially the strongest sources of stress and the most powerful defense against harmful stressors' (p. 163). As described above, in good-enough circumstances, the affective and regulatory communication between a child and their caregiving figures will be characterised by a pattern of match, mismatch and repair – a pattern that fosters a psycho-biological balance.

A significant lack of good and responsive, well-attuned care leaves a deep mark on a child's development. Deprivation and neglect were once thought to be less consequential: these could be remedied almost automatically by later corrective experiences, as though additional, good care could make up for the earlier lack. It was thought that therapy or later relational compensations could easily remedy the vulnerabilities in children who had experienced too much unpredictability and negativity. Research has long since shown that any fundamental lack of care inevitably involves too much anxiety and feelings of being overwhelmed and has a detrimental effect on a child's development. Children who grow up with 'too much lack' are never entirely reassured that there will be care in the future; they cannot count on their hunger being sated in time, or on being comforted when they desperately need it, and so on. This causes anxiety and stress. In addition to this lack of well-attuned care, some young children are also confronted with too many nasty, intrusive or unpredictable experiences; for example, when growing up in an aggressive environment, where the occasionally caring person is, at other times, unreachable or abusive.

The experiences described above are what we refer to as 'the backpack' that a child carries with them. From their earliest experiences, the child begins to acquire initial expectation patterns, which form a kind of 'blueprint' for subsequent new relationships. Without thinking deterministically or pessimistically about further development, it is clear that a backpack with mostly good experiences gives a person a more robust start in life, because it helps them to expect good care, patience, help, etc., in new relationships as well (in the nursery or kindergarten class). A good start will last a long time, and good early development increases resilience. A good start does not guarantee optimal development at all times, though, but it does increase the chances of getting back on a better developmental track in less optimal periods. A backpack with more negative and disruptive experiences makes one more vulnerable in that respect. This does not mean that good development is impossible, but it does increase vulnerability and developmental risk.

How early stressful experiences affect brain development

The relational and emotional processes described above are reflected in the body in various ways. The most basic and therefore essential domain in which traces of negative life experiences can be found relates to the functioning of the brain, and therefore also to the numerous processes that are controlled by the brain. Indeed, the brain of a newborn human baby is still very immature, and must continue developing for many years before it may be called a full-grown adult brain. Broadly speaking, the brain can be divided into four parts: the brainstem, the cerebellum, the limbic system and the cortex. It is organised from the inside out, just as a house with ever-increasing complexity can be built on top of an old foundation.

Before and during the first few months following birth, there are important developments in the brainstem and the cerebellum that enable the baby to fulfil basic bodily functions and find a balance. In a stable caregiving environment, the baby can optimally regulate its body temperature, heart rate, breathing and blood pressure. In states of stress and arousal, such as hunger, cold, intense boredom or loud noise, this system becomes disrupted. Caring parents then help to reduce the anxiety and stress again. Once regulated again, the baby's system calms down. However, in cases of neglect, abuse or maltreatment, or following exposure to violence and crisis, the child's stress response system is overloaded too soon and too often. In such circumstances, the child is deprived of the calm state that is crucial for the optimal development of the regulatory systems that function via the brain.

Too much stress in the first months of a child's life causes a flood of changes, both in receptors (architecture) and in sensitivity, and in the performing function of the brain. The earlier the child is exposed to too high doses of stress, the more basic the functions involved in the damage. In cases of severe and early traumatic stress, damage can occur at every level of brain function. This leads to symptoms such as increased stress reactions, sleep and attention problems (brainstem); difficulties with fine motor control and coordination (cerebellum and cortex); social and relational difficulties (limbic system and cortex); and speech, language and learning difficulties (cortex).

This explains why complex trauma can lead to problems in various areas of development and life. We cannot simply say about children: 'What doesn't kill them will make them stronger'. The idea that a child 'has the necessary resilience, and grows from it' is similarly not entirely correct. Of course, a child is still flexible and resilient. At the level of the brain, too, a young child has remarkable neuroplasticity. However, this should not allow us to ignore the increased risk of later difficulties as a result of early trauma. Indeed, such trauma transcends the incredible capacities of resilience and neuroplasticity.

The brainstem is responsible for the core regulating functions, such as body temperature, heart rate, breathing and blood pressure, and consequently influences the sleep-wake rhythm, determines how quickly the person experiences physical stress, and how quickly their appetite and diet become involved in increased stress. The cerebellum and limbic system are responsible for the emotional responses that drive our behaviour, such as fear, hate, love and joy. The cortex regulates the more complex and higher human functions, such as speech and language, abstract reasoning, planning and decision-making. The cooperation of these domains is similar to what happens in a symphony orchestra. Because each domain has its own functions, there is more than one system responsible for the 'music' a person creates. Each domain of the brain makes a contribution, in interaction with other brain areas. In addition, each brain area has its own specific memory.

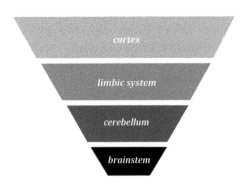

Figure 2.1 Simplified representation of the four main brain structures.

Every child is unique: the symphony that a particular child has become

Resilience should therefore be understood differently from the superficial notion that 'early experiences do not have a (lasting) impact on the young child'. Resilience means that the child – in their own unique way – tries to continue to develop as well and as constructively as possible, given the circumstances and with the talents and strengths that they possess. For example, some children who have experienced complex trauma become successful at school, or excellent performers in a given domain that interests them, while in other areas they remain vulnerable and find it difficult to have close and lasting relationships. It's not possible to predict in which developmental domain a child's vulnerability will manifest itself the most. Indeed, whereas it is possible to look at the past to understand which domains or aspects of development are vulnerable, and which point to strong resilience, it is much more difficult to predict anything regarding the future. Notions such as 'equifinality' and 'multifinality' help us to understand this. Multifinality means children can take different developmental paths from similar early traumas, and even within the problematic pathways, there is a large variation. Equifinality means that, even with different backgrounds and/or life histories, children's development in a specific domain (e.g., school attainment) can still end up at the same point.

The interplay among the various areas of development, like in an orchestra, will lead to a unique and personal 'piece of music', which will be the child-in-development. Each child is a unique symphony, in which various aspects of talent and practice come together. Each child finds their own unique way with what they have inherited and have experienced; given their own vulnerabilities and talents, each child has created their own path with these building blocks. In some of the aspects and examples described above, the reader may recognise a child in their immediate environment, while other aspects are unrecognisable. All this requires immense flexibility and resources from parents, educators and mental health professionals around such children, as the way in which caregiving adults engage with these children has a major influence on their subsequent development. An important factor in a caring and educating approach is what we refer to as 'reflective capacities': the ability – given the often difficult circumstances in which these children bring their carers – to keep reflecting about the child and about themselves (see Chapter 4). Indeed, from the perspective of the child and the care context, it is important to get a good picture of which developmental domains are the child's most intact and strongest, as these often determine their resilience for life. In addition, it is equally important to get a clear picture of the most taxed or damaged developmental domains; these are the ones most affected by the trauma. It is then necessary to look for potential growth in these areas, or – in the event of limited growth capacity – how a child can be helped to compensate for vulnerabilities by focusing on their more robust capabilities.

At this point, we want to mention the four major developmental domains impacted by complex trauma. In part 2 of this book, we will elaborate each domain in terms of the possible consequences trauma can have on a child in that domain, as well as how these can be dealt with so that growth and development can be further supported. The main themes that come to the fore in the broad research and clinical literature are all equally crucial for someone to grow into a well-functioning person. These are: (1) being able to experience and express aspects of an inner world; (2) being able to regulate stress, arousal and emotions; (3) being able to develop trust and reciprocity in relationships; and (4) being able to develop a coherent and essentially positive sense of identity. We discuss these in four separate chapters, pretending for a moment that these developmental domains can be separated from each other. Of course, this is only possible in theory. In reality, they are inextricably linked and continually influence each other.

Before elaborating these four domains in detail (in part 2), we first outline the importance of developing attachment within a relational context (Chapter 3), as well as the importance of the reflective network around children who have experienced complex trauma (Chapter 4).

3 Developing attachment is building personality

DOI: 10.4324/9781003155645–5

From regulation to attachment

During the course of their first years of life, children build up an image of what caregiving figures are like. They do this on the basis of countless minor experiences, as described earlier, for example: 'When I cry, daddy comes to see what I need. He gives me a bottle and strokes my cheek', or 'When I hold my arms up to grandma, she usually understands straight away what I mean. She then picks me up and throws me in the air until I squeal with delight'. The succession of these and similar daily experiences gives a child the opportunity to form images of adult caregiving figures as available and caring persons: 'They are there for me when I need them. They are reliable, they do what's best for me'.

Attachment development takes a completely different course if, for a significant period, the child grows up in an environment that cannot offer such availability and reliability. There may be circumstances early on in a child's life whereby the 'normal' but crucial experiences, as described above, are lacking. 'I cry because I miss my mummy so much, and there is only an unfamiliar face above my cradle'. Or 'I've been bored for quite a while. Now I'd like to play a little, but nobody has time for me'. Or 'Nobody notices that I'm terrified in the dark, I'll try to rock myself to sleep'. The child then builds up a different image of adults, for example: 'Avoid them, because they give you extra stress with all their unpredictability'. Or the child panics when an adult displays a caring side, because this – in the child's mind – means that there will be a price to pay as soon as something goes wrong.

The fact that attachment is often central in cases of complex trauma is no coincidence. Complex trauma undeniably has an immense impact on attachment and subsequent personality development – to such an extent that, as described earlier, authors sometimes speak of 'attachment trauma' (Allen, 2013). Attachment is an important and widely used theoretical concept that helps us to understand what we described earlier. However, and especially when it comes to children traumatised at any early age, 'attachment' is used as an umbrella term, as though everything is explained when we say that a child is 'showing a vulnerable attachment development' or has an 'attachment disorder'; and as though everything is resolved as long as we provide enough 'corrective' attachment experiences.

Attachment development as a lifelong process of growth and maturation

As aptly stated by Allen (2013), 'we can understand best the profound significance of attachment relationships by viewing them as embedded in our lifelong quest for psychological maturity' (p. 3). In other words, attachment development is part of an individual's lifelong process of growth and maturation towards adulthood. This growth process takes place within one's closest relationships. Every person has to deal with two developmental tasks throughout life, which are interwoven and constantly require a new balance (Blatt, 2008, p. 3). This is the development of

1 the way we relate to others, how we learn to engage in and maintain mutual, meaningful, personal and fulfilling relationships. In children, this is about shaping long-lasting relationships with parents, grandparents, siblings, friends, and so on; about falling out and making up again; about feeling loved in spite of one's vulnerabilities and little flaws, and so on;

2 the way in which we build up a coherent, realistic, differentiated and integrated sense of self in which the positive feeling predominates and is maintained or found again, above and beyond negative experiences. This sense of self plays an important role in how we develop our lives. In children, it is about how they discover what their talents are, and how they hold on to them and shape them. Trying out hobbies and discovering that some hobbies 'grab' them, while other activities do not really interest them.

In this balance between relatedness and autonomy, every person, at any point in their development, has the tendency to be more inclined to one side than the other, based on the very personal interplay of aptitude and experiences. One person finds energy in organising a family celebration, the other in being alone and being able to work on a painting. In one period of life, one can be highly focused on an important project, such as running a marathon or writing a doctoral thesis; in another period, one invests in and primarily gets energy from taking care of children, family or parents.

This balance is therefore by no means a static given. As every tightrope walker knows, balance can be maintained precisely by a succession of continuous minimal movements, whereby the counter-movement serves to restore balance after the previous movement (see also Phillips, 2010). As such, following a period of hard work, a person may be looking forward to getting back to their family; or, after a long holiday looking after the children, one may yearn to get back to work and their own projects.

This lifelong, two-pronged developmental task starts within the very first relationships the child enters into, as soon as it is born. Children practise engaging in relationships from the start of life, with parents and the broader (family) context playing a crucial role in this relational development. In this chapter, we once again require some developmental thinking to explain the important role new caregiving figures can have in a child's life; how foster carers and adoptive parents or residential care workers can help vulnerable children develop in better, healthier, more flexible, more mature ways. We describe how children within this relatedness also need to find space to be able to 'do their own thing' – in other words, to 'explore', in the broad sense of the word; to discover parts of the world and of themselves, independently of their parents. We then elaborate what it means when these developmental tasks originate in a parenting environment that – for whatever reason – has not been sufficiently caring towards a child. Finally, we explain how seriously maladaptive attachment development – also sometimes referred to as an 'attachment disorder' – can be understood as the best possible adaptation to the given circumstances. Often, it is precisely the new circumstances that make visible and tangible what relational and autonomous skills a child has built up and where they fall short in the new, more caring environment. At the difficult start of life, the child's built-up pattern of coping mechanisms and relationship modes helped to sustain, survive and self-preserve. This relationship pattern cannot simply be set aside as soon as the child is in a more favourable environment and becomes either limiting or inadequate.

The caregiver: from secure base to safe haven

From birth, a baby is equipped with skills that enable it to obtain and maintain the proximity of caring adults, such as crying and laughing, seeking eye contact or looking away (see Chapter 2). In addition, nature has endowed the baby with certain physiognomic characteristics, such as its big eyes, peachy baby skin and typical baby smell, which ensure that adults will be close by. Nature has taken care of this, as emotional, overjoyed and loving parents, grandparents and other caregiving figures have the urge to care for the child, provide the necessary closeness and protection, and keep an eye on how the child is doing. After all, a child is less exposed to various dangers when around adults who are bigger, stronger and wiser. Bowlby, the founder of attachment theory, called this aspect of development 'a secure base' or 'a safe base' for good reason. The Latin word *securus* means 'without worries'. In good-enough circumstances, life starts as a phase in which the child can be relatively worry-free, without intrusive and overwhelming hunger, pain, fear or cold, etc., provided that there are caregiving figures available who will take care of their worries in these first days and weeks of life, and meet their needs sufficiently. Available human presence and proximity are therefore just as crucial as eating and drinking. It is the countless minor experiences of good care, as described earlier, that give the child the opportunity to build up an expectation pattern.

As babies grow, they can gradually start going without mum or dad for a while. Caregiving figures are no longer just the 'safe base where it's good to be', they also stimulate separation and exploration as a natural part of growing up. Caregiving figures evolve from the secure base to the 'safe haven' where children can refuel. The Latin word *salvus* means 'unharmed' or 'preserved'. The safe haven is the place where the child can come home unharmed and preserved – a place where they can feel completely safe for a while, before being able to face life's demands once again and explore new situations and new relationships.

Although a child engages in a relationship with the primary caregivers from birth, we only refer to them as having an attachment relationship from the age of seven to eight months old. From then on, the child is active and clearly focused on having or maintaining a privileged contact with a particular attachment figure. Prior to that, as long as the baby was almost 'at one' with its caregiving environment, the attachment was so self-evident that it was not really a theme in the child's experiential world. After all, the child was still part of the very close physical bond with the primary caregiver. Somewhere halfway through the first year of life, the child is ready for autonomous activity – no matter how small – and the lasting connection with the person from whom they begin to differentiate becomes important. That is why attachment becomes visible from then on. As soon as autonomy development starts, the child's sense of security stemming from within the attachment relationship becomes apparent: the child knows they can rely on the caregiving figure when they get into trouble while exploring (crawling under the table, getting stuck between the chair legs) or become frustrated (the box that refuses to open, while that nice little shape is inside it). After calming down and refuelling on confidence from the caregiving figure, the child can go on their way again and seek autonomy.

From the age of seven to eight months, games of reciprocity start to appear; in which the child laughs at daddy, for example, thus involving him in a game of looking and then looking away, laughing and pulling faces, etc. It's no coincidence that peekaboo becomes the child's favourite game during this phase of life. Conversely, a child turns away when a stranger gets too close. In other words, they become 'shy' during this period, meaning that they only allow themselves to be comforted by those few familiar people, not by everyone. They start to show 'stranger fear' or 'eight-months fear'. The child barely tolerates being picked up by a stranger; they sometimes can't even bear the fact that a stranger is looking at them. Attachment has developed and this soon becomes clear from the child's – sometimes very exclusive – preference for the attachment figure. The child cries when the mother leaves; they long for the father when they feel uncomfortable, or when they have fallen and are in pain. In other words, the attachment relationship is the relationship with the preferred, exclusive caregiving figure(s) who is/are often in the vicinity. A distinction is made between familiar and safe, on the one hand, strange and frightening, on the other.

It is no coincidence that at this stage, the child also discovers that they can become attached to a cuddly toy, a doll or a blanket – a predictable object, the scent or softness of which can evoke a sense of familiarity and consolation to make up for the brief absence of the actual caregiving figures. Gradually, a feeling of attachment to the caregiving figures is created; a reassuring feeling that the caregiving figures always show up again, that moments of separation are survivable and that one can fall back on the caregiving figures in times of stress, pain and sorrow. A sense of 'inner safety' is created – a safety that the child carries within themselves – even when the caregiving figure is not there in person for a while. As such, Bowlby (1973) referred to an 'internal working model'; an image that a child holds within, which can be evoked in the event of the real, physical absence of the caregiving figure. The child learns to distinguish which adults will be there for them in all circumstances, while also supporting the child's exciting urge to explore and acquire autonomy.

The fact that experiences with caregiving figures repeat themselves leads to the construction of a kind of 'script', an expectation pattern or a blueprint of how relationships work. In good-enough circumstances, a child learns where they can find comfort and help, because they have experienced countless times that mum and dad, grandma and grandpa, and later also the child nurse or the kindergarten teacher, are there for them. A kiss from mum on a grazed knee, or daddy doing a thumbs-up as encouragement in the midst of the pain of the grazed knee – these are the miracle remedies in the event of pain or fear, provided the child feels safe in these relationships. A child whom we call 'securely attached' is a child who, in the event of fear and discomfort, or when they feel alone, has been given opportunities to experience finding peace in the proximity of caring adults. The child can refuel there in order to refocus on what they were doing.

A secure attachment relationship as a foundation for healthy emotional development

The fact that a child becomes 'securely attached' means the balance between being focused on the caregiving figure (relatedness) and being focused on the environment (autonomy) is in relative equilibrium. The fact that the child can 'refuel' with peace of mind when they have ventured a little too far, or when they need their attachment figure, or just to share and show what they have found in the world during their curious voyage of discovery, makes it possible for them to go off on their own again with a safe feeling and to further develop their autonomous activities. It's all about the relatively flexible balance between enjoying being close to mummy or daddy, on the one hand, and being absorbed in play, and letting go of or 'forgetting' mummy and daddy for a while, on the other. The stronger the relationship is, the easier the child can manage separation and exploration; in other words, the stronger the elastic band, the further the child can go without the connection snapping.

When the child has been able to practise, in a safe context, going off by themselves and being left alone but always being found again, they build up the experience that separation can be survived, that autonomy is also pleasant and that the other person is still there and still interested in the background. No matter how scared a child may be when mum or dad leaves them in day care, it helps that they always show up again: an inner conviction develops that they are always there for the child. Practising with what can be expected in relationships, interacting with emotionally available and trustworthy caregiving figures, results in the acquisition of various skills that will make the child's life easier in the future, and which can be summarised as follows:

1 Safe images (representations) of and expectation patterns towards others: a securely attached child looks for the caregiving figure's proximity when wanting to share a fun experience or when not feeling great. They expect to find interest or comfort from the adult. The resulting images of available and reliable parents are then taken to other relationships. The earliest relationships provide the ingredients for the way in which future relationships (e.g., with the kindergarten teacher) are shaped and coloured.

2 A sturdy self-image: a securely attached child goes through life with a relatively strong sense of self, a conviction that they are accepted by others, that they have a right 'to be' and that others find them worthwhile; 'People treat me with care, which must mean that I am worthy of that care'.

3 Skills to regulate oneself in circumstances of mild stress or anxiety: a securely attached child has often experienced that caregiving figures help them find consolation when they are upset. They internalise these regulating actions and skills. For example, they will soothe themselves to sleep by stroking their cheek with the blanket or get over a minor graze on the playground by rubbing their knee themselves. They first learn how to regulate themselves in minor incidents, while continuing to rely on the regulating skills of the caregiving figure for larger anxieties and developmental tasks. For example, a young adult student will sometimes barely give any sign of life for weeks, but will pick up the phone to call mum or dad after a straining exam.

4 Curiosity about one's own inner world and that of the people around oneself: because others approach and treat the child as a person with an inner world filled with desires, expectations, anxieties, worries, angry feelings, etc., the child learns that behaviour is connected to what is going on in one's inner world. They gradually become more curious about their own inner world and discover that others also have an inner world that can differ from theirs. This forms the breeding ground for empathy and pro-social behaviour. In other words, the child builds up the crucial capacity of 'reflecting' or 'mentalizing' about themselves and – by extension – about others (see Chapter 4).

The range of expectations that a child builds up through their very first social relationships is similar to how one develops a mental map of the area where one lives and of the social interactions one has. This map teaches the child to distinguish the safe and quiet places from the busy or dangerous places. The map also indicates the social interaction rules that can guide the child; it contains the signs that indicate where it is safe and where danger can be expected. 'If my mummy is very tired, I'd better leave her alone for a while. When she starts talking and laughing again a little later, I know it will be easier to get her to play a game'. 'When I ask grandpa how grandma was as a mum, his gaze goes blank. But if I fool around a bit, he snaps out of it'.

Attachment in the context of complex trauma: a blueprint of anxiety and distrust

When, early in life, the child experiences that the bonds it enters into are soon broken again, or when it grows up with adults who are absorbed by their own worries, sadness or depression and are therefore not emotionally available, it builds up completely different expectation patterns and images. When caregiving figures are replaced frequently and rapidly, there is no predictable pattern to how others interact with you. One morning you are woken up with a gentle song and a kiss, and the next morning you are plucked from your bed with a silent, cold stare. The child then builds up 'internal working models' or expectation patterns of, for example, being rejected or left alone, of being punished or belittled; or they notice that when they start to expect a certain way of being cared for, this is suddenly completely (and unpredictably) different again. These working models of unavailable, harsh or unpredictable interactions become the guiding template or script that shapes the child's future relationships. The emotional absence, as well as the unpredictability of caregiving figures, causes stress for a child. In these circumstances, avoiding excessive and persistent stress is often the best possible care for the child's developmental opportunities. From an early age, children have various mechanisms at their disposal to deal with excessive relational stress.

'Always stay close to me'

When the child has primarily experienced that it is best not to lose sight of the caregiving figure, a script emerges that says: 'As long as I keep involving her, everything is fine! I mustn't lose her'. A child then wants to be in constant contact with the caregiving figure, but without ever really being satisfied and refuelled. For example, they keep a constant eye on their mother and panic when she is out of sight. They cling to their mother when she is there again, though without being comforted and reassured. The child has little in the way of independent play and autonomy, they do not have the time or the peace for it, so to speak, because they have to constantly assure themselves of a minimal amount of care from the parent: 'Is she still there?... What about now, is she still there?'

The child invests more in maintaining the bond with the caregiving figure than in their own autonomy; the focus on proximity is at the expense of exploring and developing their own sphere of interest. We refer to a child with such a relational style as a child who has 'anxious-ambivalent' or 'clinging' attachment. They are afraid of losing the caregiving figure (anxious) and at the same time easily upset or angry, precisely because they have no autonomy or too little, or don't dare to (ambivalent). The child longs for autonomy and self-determination but is afraid of losing the parent altogether (separation anxiety). In response to this anxiety, they move closer to the caregiving figure again, to be reassured of the caregiver's presence. These children are often intense in their emotional reactions.

> *As a four-year-old, Louise is still lost on the playground every morning when mum drops her off at school. Her behaviour is more like that of a baby or toddler being brought to the nursery. She doesn't seem to develop any preschool skills to bridge the moment of saying goodbye and separating. Only when the teacher takes her to the classroom do things calm down again. But even in class, she doesn't start playing. She needs the teacher a lot, to stay close by.*

'Better to be near me at a distance'

In the same search for balance between relatedness and autonomy, the child may also have learnt that it is better not to appeal to the caregiving figure to be too close, because they might then lose the caregiving figure altogether. At first sight, such a child does not seem to care too much whether or not the mother is close by. Instead, they seem to focus mainly on 'going their own way': they are busy with toys, activities and their environment; they move around at a distance from the caregiving figure, avoiding physical contact and emotional proximity. When the mother disappears from view and returns, the child pretends to barely notice. It is important to bear in mind that this is only a strategy they have developed: the child has learnt that clinging to the mother and showing they want her nearby is pointless and only drives her further away. These children experience as much stress in moments of separation as the anxious-ambivalently attached children. However, these well-controlled and unemotional children more likely express their stress in an increased heart rate and other physical stress parameters. They are referred to as 'avoidantly attached' children because they have learnt that contact at a distance is the best possible strategy. The child focuses mainly on their own activities or autonomy, not because they have confidence in the other person, but to avoid the painful feelings of not being able to rely on the other person. In this way, the child manages to avoid the pain of being left alone. Like clinging, avoidance is a strategy for putting as little strain on the attachment relationship as possible, given the circumstances.

These are children who sometimes long for relatedness, but at the same time are so afraid of engaging in it. They are more likely to fall back on themselves than on the caregiving figure. They show little emotion outwardly, because emotions would make them more dependent on the caregiving figure. That is why they become 'thinkers' rather than 'feelers', who often manage to fall back on themselves.

This autonomous side seems to be a strength in childhood, but subsequently or in other contexts (e.g., in a foster or adoptive family), it seems that they have not learnt to rely on caregiving figures and also cannot tolerate being approached by adults or being offered care by them.

> *In learning to ride his bike, Martin falls off again and again. The fact that he gets up each time without crying and tries again, makes those around him think he is a 'brave little man'. Only later do his parents realise that Martin had no idea that he could fall back on them for comfort, help or support at such moments.*

'I have no idea how close I want you'

The anxious-ambivalently attached and the avoidantly attached children still have a consistent relational style or strategy: the first group is strongly focused on contact, the second acts standoffish. However, the child may also have learnt that there isn't really an appropriate strategy towards the attachment figure. A pattern of inconsistent care leads to an expectation pattern of unpredictability and anxiety. At times, the child reacts by clinging; at other times, they reject the caregiving figure. At times, they look after the parent or cheer them up and reassure them; then, they boss them around and scold them, putting them in their place. The child cannot find peace, either at a distance from the caregiving figure or in his or her vicinity; they constantly change strategy hoping to experience some sense of control, but no level of proximity or distance affords the child peace. Children who do not find a consistent way of dealing with the tension of relatedness and autonomy are at increased risk of problematic development. Indeed, going through life without a map entails chronic stress. Neither proximity nor distance offers a sense of safety. The child continually 'switches' between the fear of being left to fend for themselves versus the constant level of stress that is generated as soon as they enter into a relationship. The price the child pays in this regard is that a more vulnerable foundation is laid, on which feelings of loneliness, fear of loss, etc., grow more easily, and in which stress and anxiety are more often and more intensely present. We refer to a child with such an unpredictable way of relating as having a 'disorganised attachment' style.

> *When his adoptive mum takes Stephen to basketball, it's always an intense moment. He clings to his mum, then pushes her away, curses and spits at her and then throws himself back into her arms. Once calmed down, Stephen realises that he can't treat his mum like that, but in the heat of the moment he's powerless to stop it. As soon as he can throw himself into the sport, that intense moment is forgotten again. After all, he is a good basketball player who gets a lot of satisfaction out of his sport and is a good team player.*

After being with his new family for a while, a child such as Stephen can establish himself fairly well in his autonomy: basketball goes well, he has a talent for it. The other line of development, that of relatedness, is more vulnerable. With Stephen, this becomes clear in public, at transitional moments at the sports club. With many children who have experienced complex trauma, this dynamic remains hidden, despite their good development in hobbies and at school, and only shows itself indoors. In the seclusion of the attachment relationship with the new foster carer or adoptive parent, some 'ghosts from the past' resurface, sometimes sporadically and to a limited extent. However, in some children – and the longer they have been part of the family – this becomes increasingly intense or even unmanageable. As aptly expressed by Casement (2002), 'a sure way of getting lost, is to rely on a familiar map in unfamiliar territory' (p. 110).

A new map?

> *We left our maps,*
> *somewhere, not angrily, not wistfully;*
> *they told us what we already knew,*
> *where we came from,*
> *not where we were.*
>
> **Translated from the poem 'Verder'**
> **by Rutger Kopland (1982, p. 12)**

Of course, there are various ways in which early relational insecurity is experienced by a child and is reflected in relational scripts, expectation patterns or attachment styles. Some children have greater resilience and protective factors, such as a milder temperament, at their disposal. Or they benefit more from later well-attuned family experiences or from a therapeutic process to gain a basic sense of safety and trust. Unfortunately, there are also foster and adopted children in whom these 'ghosts of early childhood' seriously undermine or even render impossible the attachment possibilities in the new family. In the next chapter, we will explain how the network can help the child to make a new map, based on the social interaction in the new family situation. In Chapter 7, we further elaborate on how such expectation patterns can also be challenged in psychotherapy, so they do not continue to function as fixed fearful and distrustful relationship templates. Psychotherapy aims to gradually make room for more positive relational expectation patterns, aside from the sometimes tenacious negative expectation patterns.

4 Need for reflective parents and network

DOI: 10.4324/9781003155645–6

Learning to think about one's inner world happens within 'normal' family interactions

A child growing up in a safe environment feels treated and approached as a developing person with feelings and needs, wishes and desires, worries and anxieties, irritations and anger, etc. With the help of caring adults, they will learn to distinguish between minor stress and genuine fear, between being playfully frightened and actually being afraid of the dark, of being alone and of not being able to do something. They first recognise different basic feelings such as fear, joy, anger and sadness, and gradually learn to understand more nuanced feelings such as disappointment, sympathy, forgiveness and so on. They experience first-hand what these emotions feel like, and then learn the words with which to label them. The attention that parents and other caregiving figures pay to their children's inner world helps children to become curious about their own inner world and that of others. It also helps to further develop their own inner world into a more complex, nuanced world with a wide range of differentiated emotions. Parents and caregiving figures do not have to follow any training for this, they do so on the basis of spontaneous and intuitive processes in the context of the self-evident nature of daily life. Typical family conversations at the dinner table or in the car provide the most fertile ground for developing 'mentalizing' skills. This is often about what intentions we have ('I would like to play a game later on'), what intentions others have ('First I have to go to the shops, but then I can play with you') and how we can take each other's intentions and expectations into account ('Okay, shall we play together after dinner?').

In addition, the playfulness that characterises normal family interactions is a second important breeding ground for developing mentalizing skills: 'Don't you feel like finishing your plate? Come on, one more bite for grandma!' Or 'Look, my fork is an airplane! Open your mouth, the plane is coming. Vrrrroom!' Being carried upstairs playfully, like having a piggy-back ride on daddy's back when they don't feel like going to bed yet and leaving the cosiness of the living room, helps the child deal with the fact that they must – in whatever way – take into account the demands and expectations of reality ('It's bedtime, because tomorrow is school again!').

'Mentalizing': a word used by psychologists to describe mindfully relating to children

However ordinary and self-evident these kinds of interactions may seem, they are essential in the process of growing up, in order to develop 'reflective' or 'mentalizing' skills. A child who learns to distinguish and communicate gradations and nuances in feelings can also gradually tolerate these feelings more effectively, without being at the mercy of them. For example, they learn to tolerate the fact that things are sometimes not allowed, or that they sometimes have to stop playing because it's bedtime. As soon as they are able to express dissatisfaction in a different way, they no longer need to stomp their feet when they are angry or want to get something. They no longer have to scream and shout as soon as they find words like: 'I don't want you to make my sandwiches, I can make them myself'. We then say that a child is developing early 'reflective' or 'mentalizing' skills: skills to understand behaviour from underlying thoughts, feelings, intentions and meanings.

The child learns all this in interactions with adults who are emotionally more mature, sensitive and wiser than the child themselves. For most children, these are the interactions with thoughtful and sensitive parents, grandparents, uncles and aunts, the kindergarten teacher or the school teacher. In the midst of these relationships, the child – almost imperceptibly – learns an awful lot about emotional and relational development:

1 They experience continuity with regard to themselves as a little person: 'I am Tina, and sometimes I am angry, but I can also be happy or just content because it is pleasant and calm around me. But I will always be the same Tina'. Predictable reactions from others are an essential precursor to this experience of continuity in self-experience. This is also called 'self-constancy'.
2 They learn to assign meaning to behaviour: by experiencing how thoughts and feelings underpin one's own behaviour, the child becomes predictable and understandable to themselves: 'I kick the table... because I am angry at the cat that tripped me up'. In the same vein, others become predictable and understandable as well.
3 They will notice that their internal experience and beliefs do not correspond to those of others; in other words, there is no such thing as one truth and one reality.
4 This capacity to mentalize contributes to a level of communication in which perspective-taking is important. In very small steps, the child learns to see and take into account the other person's perspective: 'I really feel like eating sweets, but I understand that you have said "no" because we are about to have dinner'.

5 Finally, mentalizing contributes to the experience of a relational exchange in which personal truths can co-exist and in which deeper bonds with others can develop – bonds in which different points of view can co-exist.

In other words, the development of mentalizing capacities plays an important role in daily functioning. Issues with this ability have important implications for everyday living together.

Learning to parent happens without training or a manual: parents in search of compasses

When Sam and Iris, three and four years old respectively, play together, things are fun for a while. Sam runs away and laughs when Iris chases him and tries to catch him. While running, Iris, who is faster but more clumsy, bumps into her younger brother Sam. He falls over and starts crying. 'Oh dear, that gave you a fright, didn't it?' dad says, helping Sam back up. 'It was an accident, Iris didn't do it on purpose'. Sam lets his father's words sink in for a moment, gets helped back to his feet, pulls himself together and then quickly gets back into the game with his sister.

From very early on in parenthood, parents are motivated to understand their child. Usually – because they love their child – they look for a compass to understand them. Sometimes, they reach for an external compass and read a book about parenting; most of the time, however, they fall back on an inner compass: their capacities to observe and understand what is going on in their child's inner world. Moreover, they often fall back on their own experiences of being 'mothered' or 'fathered' in a wholesome and helping way. In no other phase of life are we so preoccupied with what kind of parents our own parents were, than in the phase of early parenthood. It is as though, in our own parenting, we want to distil the bits we wish to copy and leave out the bits we would rather not repeat.

This internal compass or mentalizing ability – the ability to understand behaviour as motivated or arising from a complex inner world of desires, fears, intentions and meanings – can be considered one of the most important capacities that 'average parents' have to give direction to the way they relate to their child in small, everyday events.

When mothers are more inclined to adequately guide their child's inner world through appropriate mind-related comments, their children are more likely to develop a secure attachment at 12 months (Meins et al., 2001). The focus on these mental contents should be sufficiently attuned to the child's level of development (Bernier & Dozier, 2003; Meins et al., 2003).

Reflective capacities prevent parents from acting on the basis of an action-reaction pattern or from their own fight, flight or freeze reactions, especially at times when family stress is high. In good-enough circumstances, parents' mentalizing capacities develop alongside their children's development. Indeed, each new developmental phase requires new parental skills and support.

'The infant's sense of self develops from the "mirroring" responses of caregivers' *Allen (2013, p. 142)*

The earliest precursors of mentalizing capacities develop when the parent mirrors the young child's inner world. Indeed, babies are not yet capable of recognising and differentiating between emotional sensations in themselves. They have a limited but crucial arsenal of affective signals at their disposal. To communicate discomfort, frustration or sadness, for example, crying is the most important signal. The parent mirrors the discomfort, frustration or sadness with their own face and voice. Gergely and Watson (1996) refer to this process as 'social biofeedback'. After all, the parent does not simply bounce the child's emotion back, does not respond to fear with fear, or sadness with sadness. Rather, they magnify the emotion somewhat, and at the same time, add a soothing undertone or a comforting smile: 'Dear oh dear, all these tears! Tell Mummy all about it', or 'Woah, that was a scare, wasn't it!' The parent mirrors a somewhat exaggerated – acted or playful – expression of the child's emotion, so that distance and processing can occur. This is called 'marked' mirroring; parents use a marker pen, so to speak, to magnify their child's feelings. In this way, it becomes clear to the child that it is about their own feelings and not those of the caregiving figure. They learn that these feelings can be symbolised in a bearable way. In this social biofeedback process, the child learns three crucial skills: they learn to recognise and experience their own sensations or feelings; they learn to regulate them; and moreover, they learn to distinguish their inner world from the outside world. As long as (young) children are not yet able to recognise their own sensations as inner states, they have to fall back on their parents' mirroring to identify, from the outside in, their own inner feeling and make them thinkable and communicable. It is the parent who – in response to the child – experiences the emotion, absorbs it, regulates it for them and gives it meaning, and then returns it to the child in a recognisable, meaningful and less overwhelming way. As such, early in life, a baby depends on the caregiving figure in order to understand itself. For example, when the baby is frustrated by hunger because its bottle is not yet warm, the parent will experience this frustration themselves, and then regulate it ('It's almost warm, just a little while longer') before returning it to the child ('Isn't that a pain, having to wait like this? But the milk is almost ready, just a little longer'). Through the other person's mirroring, the child learns to know and recognise their inner sensations, to gradually name them and finally, to regulate them by themselves.

A similar process occurs later on in life. When, as adults, we are upset, it is still helpful that someone stops and mirrors: 'Are you upset? What's up?' In other words, this process of reflection and mirroring continues to play a role in regulating intense emotions throughout life. Throughout their child's development, parents often keep asking themselves what might be behind their child's behaviour and give it meaning by referring to what they suspect is going on in the child's inner world: 'He acts so tough... when he feels very insecure'. This conferring of meaning creates a different pattern of communication between parents and child, compared to when the parent reacts from the feeling: 'Listen to him mouthing off again!' In good-enough circumstances, this event is experienced as a spontaneous search process. Authors such as Papousek and Papousek (1987) refer to 'intuitive parenting', which is characterised by trial and error, based on mutual love. When you love someone you want to understand them and approach them with an understanding attitude. 'Why are you doing that?' we ask when someone we love hurts us. In other words, love is an important incentive in the desire to understand the other. Being understood is like having a mirror held up to you, so that you can understand who you are, or that helps you to give a place to what you think and feel. How different would the message be, if Sam's father had reacted with: 'Knock it off, son, crying is for wimps, just keep playing'? How much more energy would it have taken Sam to digest his scared reaction and his father's remark by himself?

Children who have experienced complex trauma are more difficult to 'read'

When children grow up during (part of) their first years of life in interaction with adults who – due to certain circumstances or problems – are unable to behave in a way that is bigger, wiser and more mature, this not only interferes with the development of attachment but also with the development of mentalizing skills. In this regard, for 30 years – since studies by Cicchetti and Beeghly (1987), among others – research has shown that children who have been maltreated have limited ability to understand emotions. There are three main reasons for this.

First of all, caregiving figures may be limited in their mentalizing capacities or may not have enough time to talk to children about emotions, as is the case with neglect (e.g., Edwards et al., 2005). In these circumstances, children have far fewer opportunities to practise understanding themselves and others.

Second, the excessive negative life experiences that these children have been confronted with have led to a chronically heightened reactivity to stress, which strains their (more limited) reflective abilities in daily life more heavily. Stress-sensitive children continue to react

Figure 4.1 Traumatised children's being more difficult to 'read'.

more sharply, more intensely, or differently to stressful situations than children who can grow up in circumstances that allow them to develop calmer and better regulated.

Third, instead of becoming curious and intrigued about themselves and others, children can switch off and become anxious about any reflection on emotions. After all, the psychological world they have encountered around them is so terrifying that they would rather not fathom it. Their desire to understand others is not nurtured but undermined. Similar to children with an autistic disorder (Baron-Cohen, 1995), children who have experienced trauma may lack the capacity to understand their own emotional inner world and that of others. In this context, there is sometimes talk of 'mindblindness' (Allen, 2007). These children sometimes do not want to dwell at all on questions such as: 'What is going on in my inner world and in that of others?' Answers to such questions would perhaps disrupt rather than foster one's own development. Indeed, questions such as 'Why did someone punish me so hard that it left me with a crushed toe?' inevitably evoke ideas in a child that will give them a sense of control and understanding of the situation, for example: 'That can only be because I am a terrible child. I guess I deserved it', or 'Why did my mum abandon me? I must have made her terribly unhappy'. In other words, sometimes it's wise for a child to stop wondering what is going on in others, because the psychological reality that they would encounter is too difficult to bear, or can only be understood by conferring negative meaning about themselves. Not only will this result in reflective or mentalizing capacities being underdeveloped; its seeds also get inhibited, out of fear of overwhelming and frightening images about oneself and others.

All this means that these children have fewer reflective capacities to think about who they are and what they experience. As a result, on the one hand, they are more difficult to read, and on the other, they are more at the mercy of the unformed emotional rollercoaster that is their inner world. Their moods are less easy to interpret, and their feelings and thoughts more difficult to understand based on what they show. Whereas most children who grow up in 'normal' circumstances become relatively regulatable and somewhat predictable throughout development, parents of children who have experienced complex trauma continue to face much longer-lasting and much more intense dysregulation and unpredictability.

Parental mentalizing under pressure

This difficulty requires a lot from parents' stress system. These parents cannot simply count on the fact that, if things go well today, there is any guarantee for tomorrow. In that respect, the time span in which these parents live is similar to that of parents of a young child, where you monitor the state of your child from moment to moment, and what he or she needs at any particular time. As a result, parents remain anxious about the less predictable aspects of their child, even in good times. They are confronted with the continual realisation that their child is different and more vulnerable, even if things are going relatively well right now. Or they hear remarks from other people, for example, the football coach saying: 'You know, last Wednesday he did so well, but today he was all over the place'. Or, as L's parents often experience, there are periods of relative calm, during which weekends go smoothly and future plans can be made. However, these periods can suddenly – without any obvious reason – turn into a crisis, in which things can go wrong anytime. Parents walk on eggshells for a long time; cautious plans for the future must temporarily be put on hold. Sometimes, parents fear that their child's future is one in which they will never grow up without chronic psychiatric care, whereas at other times, they have a more hopeful outlook.

While, on the one hand, these children become dysregulated more quickly, and on the other hand, they have fewer capacities to manage it, they have also been confronted with more experiences that require processing and mentalizing than an 'average' child has. These are experiences of early relational trauma, but also experiences of relational difficulties that occur in the here and now, and that are related to or triggered by those earlier traumas. For example, a child or adolescent who has experienced complex trauma is often burdened by social exclusion because of their special status; or a hospital admission or police intervention in crisis may be necessary at some point due to the child's complete dysregulation. In this sense, parents' reflective capacities are taxed considerably. These parents are required to be 'more than good-enough parents'.

How does a parent maintain their compass when they get caught up in the storm?

> *With Luke, I miss the spontaneous parenting I have with my two eldest children. With him, there's a lot more thought required. Inevitably, you ask yourself more often: 'Are we good parents?' With the other two children, 'loving' is enough. With Luke, loving him is not enough, he needs more. And that's difficult, because you often experience that you fail as a parent. You also often have to let go of what you previously thought as a parent, namely that you would care for an adopted child in the same way as your other children.*
>
> LUKE'S MUM

Whereas in the past it was thought that a difficult attachment development could be compensated for by providing a child with sufficient 'emotionally corrective experiences' to make up for what they had lacked previously, the emphasis has increasingly shifted to the importance of reflective skills as being crucial in raising children who have experienced complex trauma. Of course, children with a special 'backpack' require more than good-enough care; these children require parents with a special sensitivity and responsiveness to their needs. However, what these children need most of all, are parents with a great willingness to keep looking for the whys and wherefores of the behaviour at all times, as well as for appropriate responses and strategies in parenting. When it comes to a child who has experienced complex trauma, it is only partly about 'catching up on what they missed'. It is much more explicitly about creating opportunities to help understand the deeply ingrained patterns that have helped them to survive during the period of inadequate care, in order to develop more communicative and constructive relationship patterns. In other words, it is about creating space to dare to try out new ways of approaching care and dependency, distance and proximity, and so on, as well as finding other ways to manage emotional and relational challenges.

However, this is not possible without parents becoming involved in the affective and relational rollercoaster. Stress and strong emotions are similar to a pebble thrown into a pond. When the stress-sensitive, traumatised child experiences a stressful experience, their system goes into overdrive. The child immediately brings the sense of being overwhelmed into the relationship with the closest caregiving figures.

> *Mum is at home when Samantha comes home from school, and – through years of experience with her daughter – is able to pick up on Samantha's stress signals. She has developed feelers to quickly interpret and understand these signals. She hears from the way a door is slammed or, conversely, the very quiet, almost furtive steps of her daughter, that something is amiss. Immediately, her alarm system is triggered ('Oh no, something is going on, hopefully it's not too serious') and she feels how she already gets nervous about a possible new incident at school.*

In this context, Turnbull (2012) refers to 'secondary victims', the persons who fall prey to the 'ripple effect' of the stress elicited by the traumatised child's experiences. The extreme level of anxiety to which the child sometimes falls prey spreads and affects the people close to

Figure 4.2 The pebble in the pond and its ripple effect.

the child. The 'ripple effect' refers to the pebble that is thrown into the pond and makes the largest splash where it hits the water. Although the ripples in the pond are then less powerful, they often reach the edge of the pond. This is where the family members and friends who are confronted with the alienation, irritation, volatility and violence of the victims of complex trauma are.

Due to unpredictability or volatility, the interaction with the child sometimes feels like a minefield in which a seemingly low level of frustration can provoke intense conflict. As a result, the parents become hypervigilant and run the risk of chronic stress. Some parents say that they can only relax when their child is asleep, as though that is the only time they can be assured of not having to be prepared for new outbursts or unexpected escalations. Nevertheless, the path to recovery for the child, and to a liveable family balance, is primarily through the endless rediscovery and recovery of parents' mentalizing abilities. But, as we will elaborate further, this is not only the task of the parents.

Wanted: 'extraordinarily good parents' – vulnerable children require parents with extraordinary reflective skills

Parents' reflective abilities play a protective role in child development, as they increase the chances of healthy development. When parents can think about the inner world behind their child's behaviour, they offer the child, in countless minor, everyday situations, the opportunity to better understand themselves and discover their own inner experiences, thoughts and feelings. As explained, these reflective skills are particularly important for parents of children who, in their earliest years, have often experienced stressful and traumatic situations and have been confronted with definitive relationship breakdowns. Such children are more likely to exhibit behaviour that is more difficult to understand and manage, both for themselves and those around them. Fortunately, these children's development is still malleable and can be influenced, even after difficult or traumatic experiences in early childhood. At the same time, the flexibility (or growth possibility) is smaller than in a 'typical' child, precisely because the early relationship breakdowns and experiences of loss have affected this flexibility or plasticity. In addition to so-called 'corrective experiences', parents' reflective capacity is crucial in facilitating post-traumatic growth in the child.

When such children behave in a way that, at first sight, seems difficult to understand, it is crucial that parents have the capacity and energy to remain reflective. Behaviour that is 'inappropriate' or 'annoying' often expresses the child's difficult feelings. It can be an expression of feeling abandoned, of feeling overwhelmed by the loss of their previous environment, of feeling very different from their peers and family members, of anger about what is happening to them, of anxiety and insecurity about who they are and so on. When a parent can rely on reflective skills, it helps to understand the child and to distinguish between their feelings and their behaviour. Moreover, this mentalizing can serve as a compass that guides the parent's own actions. Indeed, there are no recipes or ready-made manuals for managing moments in which the complex and unclear feelings of attachment difficulties are expressed. There is no such thing as a ready-made manual for difficult, inappropriate, impolite, aggressive or destructive behaviour. Whereas being firm at bedtime is reassuring for one child, for another child, it can increase anxiety. Whereas one child finds comfort in sitting on the parent's lap during a crying fit, another child can become anxious and first needs to keep a certain distance.

Adoptive parents and foster carers often have good reflective capabilities. After all, they have been evaluated and/or trained for this before they were allowed to adopt or bring a foster child into their home. But parental reflective capacity is not a permanently developed trait that is continually present at the same level. Indeed, this reflective capacity is influenced by the circumstances: when under stress, parents suddenly start thinking about a child in a much less broad and nuanced way, compared to moments in which they can quietly reflect on what exactly is going on. Stress can be about the more 'everyday stress moments' of family life, for example, in the supermarket after a tiring day, with a lot of household chores and professional work still on the agenda. But stress can also be the result of events that one is confronted with during the course of family life, for example, when someone in or close to the family becomes seriously ill, or when someone is confronted with serious difficulties at work. In addition, a lot of children with their special 'backpack' – due to their more difficult-to-read, more negative or more unpredictable behaviour – also cause more stress than average. Children who have severe tantrums repeatedly create rushes of adrenaline in their parents and other family members. Children with severe sleeping problems require all their parents' energy, evening after evening, so that the parent can sometimes only relax when the child is fast asleep (which is invariably too late for the parents to sufficiently relax themselves). Children who, after school, need their parents for everything, or children who conversely don't seek contact during the whole evening, tax their parents in very different but equally intense ways. Yet, it is precisely this reflective parenting that has a supporting, healing and restorative influence on the child. In order for parents to keep searching for the meaning behind their child's behaviour, during many years, and to keep wondering in amazement and curiosity about what exactly is going on and how they can help their child through it, they themselves need a network that is reflective and trauma-sensitive, a network that facilitates development and supports parents.

It takes (more than) a village to raise a child (with complex trauma): a trauma-sensitive network around parents

Sometimes, you wish there was a book in which you could look up the chapter 'He forgot his towel again, what can I do about that now?' Sometimes, it's very tiring and stressful to always rely on your feelings. With the other children, I also rely on my feelings, but that's less tiring; it's not such a balancing act and I'm allowed to fail sometimes, because there's a basis there. And if I'm wrong, that's not so bad. With Luke, it is bad, I feel it's bad, or I'm afraid it's bad.

LUKE'S MUM

Precisely because there are no 'manuals', and parents can only rely on a highly energy-intensive search process that continuously requires their attention, a child who has experienced complex trauma needs so much more from their carers. It's like driving in an unknown country without a GPS to guide you through the road network: it means that you have to have your full concentration on the traffic at all times and that any moment of inattention takes you a step back. It is precisely for this reason that caregiving figures responsible for a traumatised child (in whatever capacity – as a biological parent, foster carer or adoptive parent, or in any other educational context) deserve a trauma-sensitive support network. This network ideally includes both the informal context (family and friends) and the professionals involved (school, foster care service, adoption service, post-adoption service, etc.), and sometimes also external care providers (health care, police, etc.). Indeed, when the reflective capacity of these children's parents is taken care of, the children themselves are also taken care of.

More than in 'normal parenting circumstances', parents caring for a child who has experienced complex trauma should be able to fall back on a helping network of family and friends (Seghers, 2013). A supportive social network can be a source of understanding, empathic support and energy renewal, on the one hand, and practical help, on the other. Parents experience a great need for understanding, for being taken seriously in their story and their needs, and say that they do sometimes come across this understanding, but not always.

> *On various occasions, Lia's parents have explained to her teacher how Lia can't handle unplanned and unpredictable activities at all at home. Even so, the teacher repeatedly remarks that he thinks they are very strict and inflexible when it comes to planning and changes.*

Sometimes, parents experience authentic understanding in minor gestures from people around the family, such as when the child gets invited to a sports activity or to go on a fieldtrip, even though it is well known that the separation and distance from the parents are guaranteed to create anxiety in the child. Similarly, parents experience how practical help can mean a lot. For example, godparents, an aunt or a grandparent who invite the child to stay over on a regular basis so that the parents can relax for an evening and the next morning, and recover from the pressure of continuous vigilance.

> *Teachers at Laura's school continue to look for ways to deal with any new problem that crops up. Since the special educational needs teacher introduced a behaviour card for incidents on the bus and talked to Laura about this repeatedly, her behaviour has been relatively under control. Now that she is trying to navigate her way through all the 'romances' in her class, and in so doing, disrupts the class group, the conversations with the special educational needs teacher are about having a crush and sexuality, about relationships, and about what is private and what is okay to share in a group.*

Sometimes, parents feel sandwiched between caring for their vulnerable child, on the one hand, and societal expectations with regard to children and their upbringing, on the other.

> *There are so many things to consider. I always ask myself, should I go into this? Should I make a point of this? When the after-school teacher tells me he was very rude to him again, I usually say: 'I'll sort it out at home later'. You can't do anything about it right there and then. But, of course, you have to do something about it.*
> LUKE'S MUM

On top of that, in their search for a sense of relative balance with the child, the parents have learnt to handle certain things in a way that prevents escalation. They have learnt to choose their battles and raise their children without trying to accomplish too much all at once. It is often the structure-providing and understanding football coach or dance teacher who makes it possible for a traumatised child to pursue a hobby. These supportive figures ensure that such a child is offered a place where they can gain control over themselves while playing sports and, through sports, find a social laboratory in which to keep practising what they often find so difficult: strong and lasting relationships in the midst of difficulties and conflicts.

Trauma-sensitive mental health care

> *But they (the police) must surely be able to distinguish between a family where an injured child is healing and one where a child is being damaged.*
> MARIANNE'S MUM

In addition to the greater need for support from the informal network of family and friends, caregiving figures responsible for a traumatised child have more frequent contact with the professionals involved with their child (school, foster care service, adoption service, post-adoption service, etc.) and external care providers (health care, police, etc.). There is a significant need for trauma-sensitive mental health care, due to the many reasons that have been discussed above. For example, it is important that the problems of complex trauma are recognised by mental health professionals, so that children are not treated for one complaint and problem after the other, since it is precisely the volatility of their behaviour and the multitude of problems that are so characteristic of their way of functioning.

Parents feel this need even more acutely when their traumatised child – certainly, in full adolescence – expresses their confusion about their identity and 'belonging somewhere' in an intense, unregulated or dramatic way (e.g., by running away from home, or in other acting-out behaviour). They express how it is precisely at such most vulnerable and frightening moments that they experience a lack of understanding for their traumatised child's behaviour. They feel left alone, judged or even thwarted.

> *Marianne's mother told us that when Marianne ran away from home, someone from the public prosecutor's office was assigned to carry out a family investigation, to assess whether Marianne was in a 'problematic family situation'. When the parents wanted to explain something about her background during that conversation, the expert considered this background to be 'irrelevant, what's important is now'. These parents found it particularly disappointing that someone decides whether or not to place a child in out-of-home care without understanding the context: 'If you don't find her background relevant, you don't have any insight into how something like this could occur in the first place. If you come into contact with the police in a situation like this, you expect to actually be helped; they help you find your child, they drive around in vans, and that's of course very reassuring. And you can't expect the police psychologist to be familiar with and understand trauma as well. So, that's why you start looking for literature in which you can also find it. Yes, it's a definite lack, finding support as a parent'.*

> *When faced with parents and an adopted teenager who are intensely conflicted, clinicians may have trouble maintaining a*

nonjudgemental stance; they may overlook the possibly transient nature of the crisis. Stressed by the painful affects and deep ambivalence of family members, they may wish to intervene actively to 'rescue' someone and end the distress they are witnessing. An unattuned psychiatrist, state social worker, or judge may thus simplify the task as saving the 'good' parents from the 'bad' adolescent or vice versa. In either case, intervention may contribute to family disruption since the end result is often a weakening of the adoptive placement itself, not withstanding that the child is a legal member of the family and that this membership may be the best hope of a troubled child.

Nickman et al. (1994, p. 753)

Experiences like this make it more difficult for parents to ask for help with their parenting situation.

I was already very happy that we found a psychotherapist for our daughter, and we go there every week. But I can't go and talk to someone myself every week. It's incredibly, incredibly time-consuming. In fact, you have to be there all the time. And you constantly find yourself in very stressful, hurtful and difficult situations. Then you realise that this is even more the case for your child, so as a parent you always first look for ways to continue helping your child, and only later do you feel how you have become exhausted yourself. Fortunately, I have my mother and sister to talk to, but it's not easy to find help for myself.

MARIANNE'S MUM

Treatment: from wound to scar

How child psychotherapy and therapeutic work with the parents and the network can contribute to recovery from trauma

Introduction

Our aim in the second part of this book is to use examples from our child psychotherapy practice to offer insights into what is actually taking place in the inner world of children who have experienced complex trauma, and what this means for parents and other carers. We describe how, using a psychodynamic treatment approach, we work with the children to help them find more constructive pathways that not only lead to more optimal developmental trajectories, but also enable them to deal with the sometimes lifelong scars that complex trauma can leave behind. It is not our intention to write a manual of the specific methods and techniques we use in this context, nor do we intend to describe the treatment frame within which this work takes place.[1] We simply wish to offer a window into the playroom and the therapist's thought processes. In this respect, there are three important things to know. (1) Based on the specific context of each child, we create a made-to-measure treatment frame with three tracks: one for the child, one for the parents and (where useful) one for the network. We consider the interplay among all three tracks to be crucial for treatment to be effective. (2) In direct work with the child, we use child-specific methods of communication, namely, playing, drawing and talking. (3) We constantly bear in mind that children who have experienced complex trauma have been confronted throughout their lives with difficulties and vulnerabilities in four crucial domains of development: narrative, regulatory, relational and identity development. Depending on the child's specific experiences during their unique life history so far and

DOI: 10.4324/9781003155645-7

also depending on the current developmental phase, themes from one or several of these domains may come to the foreground more strongly than others.

Our therapeutic work with these children is based on the premise that any change that can now be realised, however small it might be, may eventually lead to a much larger change in the child's later development and future perspective. Or as Adriaan van Dis said: 'As every captain knows: a ship only needs to change course by a few degrees to arrive in another port' (Knack Magazine, 18 September 2007).

A three-track treatment approach

In direct work with the child, they can start to explore their inner world of experiences. This individual frame gives the child room to experiment, in which they can play, draw, and tell us things about themes they think others will find 'crazy', 'strange' or 'incomprehensible'. The fact that the therapist is not a part of the child's day-to-day existence makes it possible for the child to talk about aspects of their personality and behaviour without it having an effect on their daily life in the 'real' world. This offers the child a certain degree of safety and security to display feelings and anxieties that they normally try to hide from the outside world, precisely because they seem so 'strange' and are perceived by that world as meaningless and irrational.

Sometimes, we prefer to offer counselling to the parents and the child together instead of to the child alone. This is the case: (1) with young children up to an age of approximately five years; (2) when the relationship between the parents and the child is still too fragile and could be compromised if the child builds up an individual relationship with a therapist; (3) when the child's verbal and expressive skills are so limited that they need their parents' 'translation' to connect with their inner world; or (4) when the child's inner world is so intensely threatening and frightening that individual direct work may have an intensely disruptive effect on the child or runs the risk of degenerating into mere repetitive and defensive play. It can sometimes happen that a child temporarily becomes more 'difficult' for those around them during the therapy process, which can put extra strain on the often already fragile bond with the parents and/or network. This is not necessarily a contraindication to undertake individual direct work with the child, but the clinician should take this into account when considering the appropriate timing for individual direct work.

At the family level, consultations with the parents and/or the whole family are intended to help family members better understand the child, so that they can respond more adequately to the child's needs and communications, thereby maximising the opportunities for further development. At the same time, parent sessions also make it possible to talk with the parents about how they can best deal with the specific challenges they face and how they can discuss these matters with their child. In the past, clinicians sometimes thought that an individual therapeutic approach could generate sufficient movement in the vulnerable developmental trajectory of a traumatised child. In recent decades, however, the literature has consistently shown that this individual model – largely inspired by work with adults – is not adequate for children, and that working together with the child's immediate and broader environment is indispensable for therapeutic effectiveness.

At the level of the network, the involvement of the wider informal and/or formal care network is often important, since these children's behaviour generates problems in a number of different contexts. Round-table consultations with everyone concerned offer a forum to think mindfully about the best ways to provide the child with a facilitating environment, in which vulnerable development can be set and kept on the most constructive trajectory possible. It is vital to create a 'shared project', with the best possible alignment and coordination of all relevant parties and organisations. The African proverb 'It takes a village to raise a child' is applicable to all children, but even more so to vulnerable children. In this context, it is important for the parents and the family that the resulting agreed-upon treatment plan is a positive and hopeful one, in which their concerns about the clear signs of at-risk development they see in their child are carefully listened to and recognised by the care agencies and other people in their informal network. 'Hope is important, because it can make the present moment less difficult to bear. If we believe that tomorrow will be better, we can bear a hardship today' (Nhat Hanh, 1995, p.41).

Direct work with the child in the playroom: playing, drawing and talking

Children not only express aspects of their inner world in language, but also in drawings and play. To discuss these matters, in this book we will use the word 'narrative' in the sense of 'expressing something'. Children tell us about the way they experience the world and about their dreams and fantasies. They do this by means of the communication abilities at their disposal. For children, 'narrating' is more than just a linguistic process, making use of words, but also involves symbolisation through play and other creative activities such as drawing. In this respect, we concur with Desmarais (2006, p. 350): 'Whilst joint play is implicated in many aspects of development, one of its most important potential consequences for the child is a sense of feeling seen, heard and understood'. Children have at their disposal three important channels of communication (play, drawing and words) to remain in touch with the things happening in their inner world and to show these things to others. Through talking, playing and drawing, they create a story about their experiences. A drawing, a painting, a clay model, a story, a puppet show or role play – all these expressions can tell us something about a child's inner experiences. This is certainly the case when the child is offered a predictable time and space (the treatment frame and playroom) within the context of a relationship with a therapist, who is trained to listen to these experiences and then reflect on them with the child. As aptly stated by Slade (1994), 'Optimally, the child's expressions are received and shared by an adult who frames them with empathy, attention, acknowledgement and validation. When we play with a child, we let the child know that we are there to be told' (p. 95).

Child psychotherapy interventions are usually play based, since play is children's language and is also the forum in which children are unavoidably challenged in all domains of life (Gaskill & Perry, 2014). For a child, play is (1) intentional behaviour expressed in visual imagery, (2) in a voluntary and pleasant way (play has no immediate purposefulness) and (3) in an environment that is as free as possible from stress and threat (Gaskill & Perry, 2014). It is crucial that the child feels sufficiently free to play out in a carefree manner the things currently occupying their attention, as well as showing the more difficult and more hidden aspects of their inner world. Play offers the child a stage on which to express what is taking place in the deeper layers of their self (Fonagy et al., 2002). By playing and drawing, a child is able to show something of the fantasies and ideas they have acquired during their life so far (Meurs, 2009).

In Chapter 5, we describe ways in which it is possible to think, search, talk, draw and play with children in the playroom as a basis for a therapeutic process, the purpose of which is to help the child to discover, get to know and understand themselves. Sometimes, it is first a matter of gaining confidence about what one thinks and feels as a child, about the things happening in one's body and mind. In this way, it is possible to build up narrative and broader expressive skills. Once one knows and understands oneself more fully as a child, one can use this knowledge to search for new ways to relate to oneself and the people around.

Core themes at play in therapy with traumatised children: 'Regulate, then relate, then reason' (Perry, 2017)

A first crucial domain (Lieberman & Van Horn, 2011; Perry, 2017) in the direct work with children who have experienced complex trauma is regulation: the development of skills and strategies to regulate oneself and one's behaviour, particularly in moments of arousal and discomfort. Children with complex trauma live continually with imminent dysregulation. When put under pressure, their affective balance quickly destabilises, which jeopardises their relationships with others and their ability to learn at school. In Chapter 6, we show how this becomes a 'biopsychosocial trap' (Shalev, 2000), which the child risks getting caught in. This means that children with complex trauma need to get to know this aspect of their personality as well as they possibly can, in order to maintain their precarious regulatory balance and make life bearable for themselves and those around them. This is the only way to keep open their prospects for growth and development and to prevent others from disengaging from relationships with them. When emerging regulatory capacities enable the first moments of calm in the troubled inner world of a child with complex trauma, it will be possible for the child to experience relatedness. In Chapter 7, we take a look at the ways in which children who have experienced complex trauma struggle with attachment and relatedness, and how they can be supported to experience themselves as a person who is capable of making connections and building bridges to the people around them. Living with a history of complex trauma also means that the child has a very different life story and has developed a very different sense of self. These children have experienced things that the people around them can hardly imagine or, at best, only know from what they have seen in movies or read in books. In Chapter 8, we reflect on how children can be helped, within a well-regulated therapeutic relationship, to (re-)discover themselves and their vitality, as well as to develop a coherent life story, in which aspects of their traumatic experiences can be recognised and framed.

To shape the psychotherapeutic processes that are necessary to allow the development of children with complex trauma to get back on track, we focus on the four crucial developmental domains depicted below.

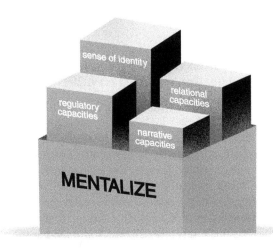

Figure II.1 The four developmental domains impacted by complex trauma, and the importance of mentalizing as the basis for intervention.

Note

1 The reader who is interested in the theoretical and technical aspects of this work and its empirical foundations can find several useful references in the bibliography and is also referred to the treatment guide to be published 'Therapeutic work for children with complex trauma: A three-track psychodynamic approach' (Vliegen et al., in press).

5 The playroom as a place for storytelling

DOI: 10.4324/9781003155645–8

Playing, drawing and talking in children
with complex trauma

> *What I most miss with Maya is a good conversation. When you*
> *ask her what her day was like at school, all she answers is 'fine'.*
> *When you ask what she did, all you get back in reply is 'all kinds*
> *of stuff'.*
>
> MAYA'S DAD
>
> *If something has happened, Luke can sometimes arrive home very*
> *upset. He can never reconstruct for himself what has actually oc-*
> *curred. You need to ask him question after question: who, what,*
> *where, when, why, how...*
>
> LUKE'S MUM

In psychotherapy, children can experience that while playing, drawing and talking, together with the therapist they can find words and
images that can be used as the carriers and providers of meaning for
their experiences. For example, a child might suddenly realise that
language can offer support, in the sense that language structures and
shapes what they think and feel. However, in the first phase of a therapeutic process, children who have experienced complex trauma often
need to go through a fairly lengthy period of 'preparatory work' before
words and images for their experiences spontaneously spring to mind.
This stems from the fundamentally different way in which these children's narrative capacities have developed. These children often find
it difficult to play, draw and tell; yet, these narrative capacities play an
important role in human interaction. The ability to express things to
other people – known as 'narrative capacity' – is one of the essential
building blocks for a number of different developmental domains. It is
our ability to tell stories that connects us with others: telling your wife
what your day at work was like, telling your parents about your day at
school, telling your colleagues what you did during the weekend. This
creates and maintains a bond with the person you tell. Telling other
people what has happened to you also helps to regulate yourself when
something has knocked you out of balance. In addition, narrative capacities are crucial for the development of a sense of self and identity:
'who am I', 'where do I come from', 'what will I become' ('a narrative
sense of self', Stern, 1989).

In children who have experienced complex trauma, narrative capacities develop in a more limited or at least different way from children who grow up in good-enough circumstances, for several reasons. The first reason for this has to do with developmental psychology: traumatised children have sometimes had fewer opportunities to 'practise' expressing their experiences with their primary caregivers. The second reason relates to the fact that these children were exposed too early and too intensely to overwhelming experiences. Intense experiences are often 'unimaginable', because they exceed our narrative capacities. When these experiences take place before we even have the words to capture and express them, as is often the case with complex trauma, this becomes even more difficult. It is such experiences that traumatised children cannot contain in language or in a story; as a result, these experiences need to find expression in behaviour, play and drawings, but in a manner that is far from symbolised or 'processed'. Consequently, these experiences remain locked in children's bodies and minds as kind of recurring nightmares, which manifest in the form of 'pop-up' jammers that destabilise a child without them or their caregivers understanding where these 'strange' thoughts, 'unpredictable' behaviours or 'odd' play contents have suddenly come from. This can result in additional difficulties for the child. For example, they may feel that significant others – parents, siblings, teachers, friends, etc. – get uncomfortable with what they do or play, because this behaviour or play reveals something of their 'wounded' – and therefore 'strange' and 'damaged' – inner world.

Narrative development: the first stories in life are 'co-constructions'

To understand exactly how the narrative development of children with complex trauma progresses differently – and more limitedly – from children who grow up in good-enough circumstances, we first outline how this development normally takes place in interaction with caregivers. In good-enough circumstances, the child's first stories are 'co-constructions'. Parents and other caregivers attach numerous words to the experiences they perceive or (in part) imagine are taking place in the child. By further building up the stories about those experiences together with the child, these experiences are taken up in a 'narrative stream'.

Joanna, a two-year-old toddler, comes home from the day nursery:
Joanna: Miranda tell book.
Mum (surprised): Ah, did Miranda tell a story from a book?
Joanna: Yes, Miffy.
Mum: Ah, the book was about Miffy?
Joanna: Yes, cocodile too.
Mum: So there was a crocodile as well?
Joanna: Cocodile cy.
Mum: Was the crocodile crying?
Joanna: Rabbet too.
Mum: There was a rabbit as well in the story?
Joanna: Yes, bad rabbet.
Mum: So the rabbit was naughty? What did he do?
Joanna (jumping up and down excitedly): Rabbet jomp mud.
Jomp, jomp, jomp!
Mum: The rabbit jumped in the mud?
Joanna: Yes. Bad rabbet! (Waving a disapproving finger in the air)
        Mud no, no!

By building (co-creating) a story together in this way, the child learns that 'a joy shared is a joy doubled', and that laughing about the naughty rabbit with mum or dad in a playful but nonetheless intense manner makes it possible to experience again and expand on the pleasure of the story's first reading in the nursery class. In the same way, the child will also learn (to complete the old proverb) that 'a trouble shared is a trouble halved': telling mum and dad about things that hurt you or made you sad can help to take away part of the pain and sorrow. By this process of 'telling', experiences and memories of events become more firmly anchored in language. As such, the child gradually acquires little nuggets of personal 'history', both about the positive moments in life ('Remember that time we laughed about the naughty rabbit?') and the more painful ones ('Remember when you fell down the stairs and cut your head? Look, you can still see the scar'.). These stories that parents construct about and with their children, in which the adults express their recognition of the child and the child's experiences as meaningful, come to serve as a holding frame, a kind of envelope in which the experiences can be preserved.

If a child cannot fall back on this kind of 'narrative envelope' during the first years of life, they will lack the foundations that encourage them to tell things about themselves, which is an important aspect of self-development. The child will not have experienced the fact that events can be shared through telling, and that this telling can be comforting or pleasant. In other words, some children have scarcely been able to experience that 'a trouble shared is a trouble halved' or that 'a joy shared' can be re-experienced, so that it becomes a 'joy doubled'. This can lead to a situation where the narrative capacities of these children are sometimes limited, even though their linguistic development is normal. In practice, this means that their 'verbal' skills can be good, in the sense of having a good vocabulary and a good knowledge of grammar, resulting in satisfactory scores when their verbal intelligence is assessed. However, this is no guarantee that the child will be able to make use of these linguistic skills to tell a story about themselves. The words they know have not become a safe haven in which past experiences or affective notions of self can be harboured; they do not form the bedrock on which the child can construct a personal life story or a sense of self.

Consequently, some of these children are less well-equipped to communicate their experiences through language and to harbour these in a story about themselves. The fact that words do not give them the bedrock they need to express the stream of experiences that are a normal part of everyday life means that these children process experiences in a different manner. This also makes it more difficult for them to appeal to others for help. This is reflected in the comment of Maya's dad, when he says that he misses having a good conversation with his 10-year-old daughter. She answers his question about her day at school with 'fine' and about what she did with 'all kinds of stuff'. This resembles the way toddlers require co-constructive support to talk about their day at school, which is still a long way from the normal conversational attributes of a child of Maya's age. Much the same is evident from the comments of Luke's mum, when she describes how her son is unable to explain what has happened when he comes home from school upset, unless she resorts to a series of co-constructive questions about the who, what, where, when, why and how. These limited narrative capacities make it more difficult for the child to feel connected to others, as is clear in the case of Maya's dad. It may also impair the child's ability to regulate and control their behaviour when they are upset, as is clear from the testimony of Luke's mum.

When experiences are too intense and come too early to be held in a narrative stream

*Fifteen-year-old Martha calls her mother following a small inci-
dent in class. They were working in groups of three on a task, and
one of the classmates asked: 'How do you spell "asymmetrically"?'
Martha says: 'With one "s"', to which the third classmate replies:
'No, with two "s's"'. Then, the first student says to Martha: 'Then,
it must be with two "s's", because you have dyslexia'. Martha (who
indeed has dyslexia) is indignant, and thinks it's mean that her
classmate doesn't take her seriously. Her mother agrees that this
is not nice, and says consolingly that Martha often knows better
precisely because she practises so hard at spelling. 'I just wanted
to get it off my chest', Martha says, ending the conversation. More
cheerfully, she concludes: 'Now, I'm going to start my maths homework. Bye!'*

In daily life, we operate from a stream of thoughts and feelings, desires, anxieties, wishes, worries and so on. These go through our minds
like fragments. We look for words and images for these thoughts and
feelings. We do this during coffee breaks at work, at moments when
we see each other again as partners or as a family after a long day in
which each went their own way. We talk about what we've all experienced and what other experiences, thoughts and memories this evokes.
Sometimes, during the course of the day, we have heard, seen or experienced things that make us happy, curious or calm; other things have
caused irritation, anger or sadness.

As in the example described above, sometimes we just need to
'get it off our chest' in order to be able to face the remainder of
the day. Sometimes, an intense experience during the day leads to
a dream that only imposes itself on us at night. Other experiences
remain completely unconscious and implicit in their influence on
us, impacting us without us ever having thought and felt explicitly
and consciously what exactly is happening. With affectively intense
experiences, the need for words can be great. When it comes to good
news, sometimes, we can hardly wait to talk about that good exam
grade, a pregnancy or an adopted child on the way, a promotion.
When it comes to negative experiences, the words are sometimes
sorely needed to give these experiences a place: from an accident we
were involved in, to a serious conflict with a colleague; from traffic

jam stress while the children are waiting in school to be picked up, to the nasty experience of an unexpected dismissal; from a child in crisis, to a parent who just received a medical diagnosis; and so on. We often tell the story several times before we feel the agitation dissipate. 'Telling is recovering', the Flemish writer and poet Luuk Gruwez explains, concisely and powerfully (De Standaard, 7 September 2012).

However, not all experiences are stored in the conscious verbal memory as 'narrative experiences'. Some experiences are so overwhelming that they leave a person speechless, making them search for words that are experienced as hopelessly inadequate. 'There are no words for this', we sigh at a great loss or intense emotion. This is true for adults, but it is even more pertinent to children whose verbal and narrative development is still ongoing. How does a baby's body feel when food doesn't come; when an undefined nasty, gnawing sensation in the belly evolves into sharp, nauseating abdominal pain, while the fear that this may happen again completely overwhelms the baby? After all, babies still have little notion of time and do not yet adequately understand the expectation that this will pass at some point. Let's try to imagine what it would be like to be somewhere completely alone, anxious and in pain, and that this happens while your psychological system has neither reflection nor language to express experiences such as hunger, pain, nausea, loneliness or anxiety. Let's just imagine for a moment that this happens when the body does not yet have the maturity in terms of muscle development and motor abilities to solve these problems by itself. It is an exercise that is difficult for us as adults, precisely because we do have language and a – relatively – mature psychological system.

When Luke came to us, he didn't dare go to sleep. That was very tiring, because you could only sit with him until he fell asleep. It took a long time before we understood why. Luke was already one and a half years old when he was abandoned. Perhaps, he could even walk at that point. That means somebody abandoned him while he was asleep, otherwise, he would have just walked after the person, wouldn't he? As soon as you realise that, you think 'it must be because he's afraid to fall asleep': 'Where am I going to wake up when I let myself fall asleep?'

LUKE'S MUM

An experience that does not become part of a narrative stream remains present in a person's body and mind as a source of disturbances that suddenly appear: 'pop-up jammers' that confront them in a dream or nightmare, in a physical or sensory sensation, or in a sudden annoying or disruptive act, with the undigested elements of the experience (see also Chapter 6). In order to properly frame and integrate experiences into a life story, a child needs adult caregiving figures around them throughout their development, who – in an almost continuous stream – give words to these 'pop-up' experiences, so that they gradually gain a place in the narrative. Children who have experienced complex trauma often end up in a vicious cycle in this developmental domain. First, the environment has more often failed in its function as a 'supportive narrative envelope', which can lead to more limited narrative capacities in the child. In addition, these children have had an overflow of intense, negative experiences, which normally require especially good narrative capacities in order to gain a place in the life story. As a result, their narrative capacity to absorb experiences into the flow of daily talking and thinking has remained too limited, making new experiences confusing, stressful and disruptive. By having so many confusing, stressful and disruptive experiences, a child with complex trauma is often chronically impaired in thinking and talking because they are dysregulated, over and over again. With a stressful mind and in a dysregulated state, one simply cannot think mindfully (see Chapter 6).

At the age of 18 months, Luke was abandoned in a residential area at night, waking up all alone, separated from his familiar surroundings without any way home. He was found and taken to a new place, to be adopted at the age of two in a new home. Such experiences are too intense, too frightening, too hurtful, too intangible, etc. for the still developing and vulnerable psychological apparatus of a very young child. The experience is then stored in the memory as a series of physical sensations, fragmented images, fragments of meaning and suddenly overwhelming affects. Luke's sleeping problems and panic reactions at bedtime prompted his parents to think that he might have been abandoned while he was sleeping. This narrative that his parents have formed around his sleeping problem is plausible, since Luke was one and a half years old when he was abandoned. One cannot easily abandon a one-and-a-half-year-old child when he's awake, without him following you. His excessive eating also raises questions.

> *When we picked him up (in his native country), we stayed with him in a hotel for a few days. There, he ate everything on his plate as fast as he could, before starting to eat our food, and other people's food in the restaurant. As soon as we got home, he only wanted to go to sleep if he could have a sandwich in his hand, so he was sure he would have something to eat the next day. [...] The last thing he would say before falling asleep was often, 'What are we eating tomorrow?' It seemed as if it didn't matter what we were actually going to eat the next day. It was more of a need to know that there would simply be food again the next day. That reassurance was what he needed to fall asleep.*
>
> LUKE'S MUM

Precisely because such experiences cannot be held in words and images, they will steer behaviour and shape relationships. Experiences that in the eyes of observers are 'ordinary' experiences – such as going to bed or experiencing hunger – can have acquired a disruptive meaning in the child's mind, triggering all kinds of survival mechanisms, such as staying alert and awake when being put to bed.

Trauma triggers: traces of trauma as jammers in play, behaviour and communication

Traumatic experiences are so completely overwhelming for a child's psychological apparatus that this apparatus ceases to function. Like a short circuit, all thinking, representing, imagining and symbolising stop, with the child desperately trying to shut out every memory or reflection. Symbolic play and metaphorical communication do not develop any further, or 'drop out', and traumatic experiences are only registered as sensory or physical impressions. As Slade (1994) stated, 'They [traumatised children] are living in a chaotic emotional universe that, by virtue of its very disorganization, precludes disguise because it precludes symbolization' (p. 89). As a result, these children often do not achieve authentic, lively and creative symbolic play, or their play is limited to 'preparing': a doll's house is tidied up and everything is made ready, over and over again, but it is never really played in. Sometimes, parents then say: 'She never plays', or 'When he plays, things get so volatile that the situation threatens to get out of hand'.

This 'short circuit' is designed to be a protective measure of the psychological apparatus against the – re-traumatising – overwhelming pain, but this measure is only partially successful. Suddenly and unexpectedly, in unguarded moments, painful and traumatic experiences break through the protective shield and manifest themselves. Similar to how, in nightmares, we are confronted with our worst fears, traumatised children sometimes suddenly find themselves in a flashback or re-enactment. When they are off-guard for a moment, they can, while playing, drawing or telling stories, suddenly express something of what they are trying desperately to keep in a closed box. Without being able to pinpoint exactly what is going on, parents feel that something 'unusual' is happening at such moments. Desmarais (2006) describes the example of a parent who says: 'I feel so uncomfortable with G's play. Characters are constantly "killed", toys are broken, it's all negative'. These brief signs or fragments of experiences can be triggered by simple sensory experiences (a smell, a look), a thought, an experience (the caregiving figure who turns their back to the child), which somehow recreate an aspect of a traumatic experience.

As a result, when playing and communicating, children who have experienced complex trauma switch between, on the one hand, moments when their play gets stuck, falls apart or doesn't even really get going and, on the other hand, moments when frightening, aggressive or catastrophic experiences come to the fore. These are two sides of the same coin: when anxiety or arousal of any kind is too high, there is a risk of a breakdown in play or communication. Too much inner chaos frightens the child so much that they stop thinking and feeling, and, as it were, pull the plug out of the socket, causing the flow of thinking, feeling or playing to stop. Too much chaos overloads the psychological apparatus and leads to a complete short circuit.

Playing is essential to growth and recovery

Under normal circumstances, children can show particularly inventive imagination in the scenes they play out. They create whole worlds while they are busy with their toys, or while they turn ordinary objects into toys. Their play shows the sensitive observer how they experience the world around them; it offers a glimpse of the themes going on in their mind. They show both their fantasies and their childlike interpretations of things they have experienced or witnessed. Acting out playful scenes is a special skill of children, in which they put themselves or part of themselves in a fantasy play, so they can portray difficult elements, frame things, communicate and change things. Jean Piaget, a cognitive psychologist, described a child's ability to depict their world, showing how they think about themselves and others while playing. Paediatrician and psychoanalyst Donald Winnicott elaborated on this perspective: in a playful way, the child not only shows how they imagine or re-enact their world; in the repetition of play, the re-enactments and images about themselves and others can evolve – especially when the child is offered a safe frame to show these images, and meets a therapist who helps them tolerate and mitigate (transform) these images and make them meaningful in the light of the questions and difficulties the child faces. Or in Jenkinson's (2001) words: 'There must be a key person who values and sanctions children's play and accepts the child's inventions with respect and delight. There must be a place for play, a "sacred space" (no matter how small), and time' (p. 137).

In the playroom, children create a kind of 'performance': in a drawing or in a play scene, deeply felt experiences can then be expressed. These scenes are always connected with the meaning of or a truth about their existence. Within a child psychotherapy process, we consider the themes that a child brings up in their play as the symbolic expression of what is going on in their thinking and feeling. The ability to re-enact these things is crucial for the child's future development: through play, they can revisit experiences or events, regain control of their anxieties and play out new roles that they would not normally be able to play in reality. Slade (1994) describes how play has several functions: (1) In play, the child creates a story, a narrative in which they weave together fragmented and incomprehensible elements (puzzle pieces of experiences) into a more or less coherent story or theme. (2) In play, a child frames experienced affects that can be modulated and integrated while playing and telling stories. (3) By playing together with the therapist, a trusting working relationship can develop between the child and the therapist. (4) By playing, the child develops reflective abilities: they learn to think about themselves, to look at themselves, to make explicit what they find important and why this is so.

Traumatised children do not always have the ability to process experiences through play and drawing. The ability to playfully deal with reality ('playing and reality', Winnicott, 1971) is more limited in children who are very anxious or who go through life with traumatic injuries. Although playing could contribute to transforming these anxieties and painful experiences, traumatised children sometimes find it harder to let themselves go in play, for fear that the full traumatic memories will immediately come to the fore and overwhelm them before they have the capacity to bear it or process it.

In order to engage in play, all children need a safe frame (Jenkinson, 2001). Adults may need to be in the vicinity or in the background. In therapy, the therapist needs to be more sensitive, providing a specific (therapeutic) relationship. The play offers children opportunities to discover and use their imagination. Although in principle this is also the case for traumatised children, it is not so easy for them to discover and learn through play: the imagination process is sometimes interrupted (breakdown in play); the child runs away, as it were, from the images they bring into the playroom, because these are too painful or too threatening.

Children also want privacy for their play; adults should not simply impinge on the play world with their own world. Just think of how a child sometimes suddenly stops playing, when it realises that an adult is watching and following along. In therapy, this privacy is created by the continuity of the frame, the predictability of the therapist and the relationship they offer, and by the personal drawer or box in which the child can put things for safekeeping. By playing, the child can experiment with a new sense of self and create things. In traumatised children, this new and creative aspect is sometimes problematic for a long time because the traumatic aspect still predominates. These children need time before they can experience that allowing different streams to influence their play can be a fun, creative activity. Until then, they are more often inhibited in play or repeat the same play over and over again (repetitive play).

Searching for words and images

Slade (1994) wrote about the essence of play therapy with the most severely traumatised children: 'With children who cannot play coherently and meaningfully, who cannot use the symbols of play and language to make sense of their emotional experiences, who cannot create narratives for their experiences, an essential and prior part of the work of treatment is to help them do so' (p. 81). However unusual or taxing the 'pop-up jammers' described above may be for the child and those around them, there are also opportunities for the child here. Indeed, a therapist does not have direct access to the trauma that the child went through, but they can work with these 'traces' or 'signs', which bear witness to the enormous force the trauma exerts on the child's psychological apparatus and that come into the therapy room like odds and ends. It is these signs, these little 'fragments of experience' that guide the therapist. When, in child psychotherapy, a foundation is created in which these signs and fragments can be contained within a reliable therapeutic relationship and a developing and growing psychological apparatus, these fragments of experience grow into islands that take on meaning within the conscious verbal memory.

These fragments and signs of traumatic experiences are sometimes expressed in images (drawings, play or behaviour) rather than in words or stories. As such, we first of all reflect on these images with children or help them find the images with which to express experiences before they can be incorporated into a flow of words and made more bearable. They become like the difficult or painful bits of a story in a book or a film: they no longer remain the 'crazy' or 'bizarre' images in the child's head and 'strange' sensations in their body that occasionally take over their entire thinking, feeling and behaviour. In therapy, we invite children in the playroom to search for words and images for what they are experiencing, what they dream of and desire and what they are afraid of. We let them experience that finding images and words can help to contain sensations, thoughts and feelings that repeatedly, suddenly and intensely disturb their daily life, in a foundation of language, in a more coherent story about themselves.

This process is hard work for the child, the parents and the therapist; after all, it is accompanied by intense anxiety, overwhelming sadness, rough, raw and primitive feelings of anger and hatred, along with the fear of going mad, being torn apart or falling apart into pieces.

Sometimes, there is first and foremost, the 'fear of words', as 10-year-old Maya shows when her mum tells the therapist Maya had a nightmare. Maya stands behind the puppet-show screen, with her hands on her ears. She doesn't want to hear anymore, a bit like Munch's depiction in his painting *The Dead Mother and the Child*. It is no coincidence that Munch was a painter who expressed many elements of early and nonverbal trauma in his work (Bischoff, 2016). He poignantly depicts how, as a child, you would only wish you could shut out these painful experiences by covering your ears. In this sense, child psychotherapy is also the continuous search for the precarious balance between helping the child to shut out what is too much and too overwhelming, on the one hand, and helping them reflect on this difficult experience, so that some incipient processing is made possible, on the other hand. It is the search for cautious balances and guarding them in the midst of bubbling-up rough and raw, primitive feelings of hatred, anger, envy and so on – feelings that children in their vulnerability often really don't want to feel, preferably, ever again. And the harder they shut out these feelings, the harder they are suddenly and unexpectedly surprised and overwhelmed and find themselves 'suddenly' in a situation of shouting and raging, or of shutting down and becoming unreachable. The trauma has to be shut out in order to survive, but it also has to be approached because, otherwise, survival will be permanently accompanied by these disruptions and 'signs' of threat. As a therapist,

Figure 5.1 Part of Edvard Munch's painting *The Dead Mother and the Child*.

and together with a child and their family, you walk a tightrope over an abyss of primeval and overwhelming affect, and struggle with how you can use the child's words and images to guide you through the impending chaos in such a way that you do not – together with the child – fall off that rope.

A drawer, a box and a sketch book as 'containers' for experiences

Because these children often have a very fragile sense of self, and also find it difficult to situate themselves in time and space, the solid frame of the playroom – in which a therapeutic process takes place – provides a helping framework within which these children can learn to think and talk about themselves. In this therapeutic frame – a predictable playroom and a fixed time – they can learn to feel and talk about how they are growing up and developing, and about how they perceive and engage in relationships. Since these children are often less familiar than other children with the experience of being able to

organise and hold experiences and events in mind, therapists tradi-
tionally offer the child a personal drawer in a cupboard or storage
box that symbolises and helps to contain and organise thoughts and
feelings. This personal drawer or box, which contains a sketch book,
is intended to store the drawings and crafts that children make during
therapy. The drawer, box and sketch book symbolise the 'containing'
presence that the therapist strives to be for the child and help the child
to experience continuity with themselves, for example by occasionally
looking in the drawer at what they have already created and stored in
therapy. For children with limited capacity to think about themselves
and what is going on in their inner world, this symbolic way of keeping
(together) thoughts, feelings and things they have made is often very
helpful. A drawer fills up over time, and every time a child rediscovers
in the drawer the things they have previously made, they also learn to
look at them as expressions of themselves and give them meaning. The
drawings and other things, as well as the meanings they are given, can
then become part of a narrative about the self, built up in the presence
of the therapist.

Becoming the director of one's story: playing and telling is also repeating, mastering, controlling

> *Finding a nest in a forest of beautiful words,*
> *sleeping in the branches of a language.*
> **Translated from the poem 'In een bos' by Marleen de Crée**
> **(2011, p. 147)**

Among other things, an experience becomes traumatic due to the
complete loss of control and the accompanying overwhelming powerlessness. For example, a child who was abandoned somewhere without
their opinion being asked, and without being able to foresee or understand what was happening. A child who was adopted, even though
they had told their sister that they didn't want to be. The scars on a
child's arms remind them that they were once severely hurt, without
being able to stop it, and without being able to remember anything
about it. After such trauma, regaining control is a crucial aspect of
processing traumatic events. On the one hand, regaining control requires a therapist who stays in control, and who helps ensure that the
child in the playroom isn't overwhelmed or hurt again. This relates to

the child's need for a therapist who is 'bigger, wiser and stronger' and who will not allow anything too overwhelming to happen to them. On the other hand, where possible, the therapist gives the child the reins. To the extent possible, a therapist makes the child the director of their own play and the therapeutic process.

With this restored sense of control, the child can start to act out scenes again: in a playful way and within the safe relationship with the therapist, in a bearable way and via the detour of signs and images that help to re-enact aspects of the traumatic experience ('Szenische Erinnerung', Grünberg & Markert, 2016). In this way, the trauma is depicted. This re-enactment in signs and images is a form of repetition in the therapeutic sense of the word: repetition makes it possible, for the first time, for the child to begin to frame and process a difficult event. Repeating sometimes happens in symptoms; for example, when the child wants to run away from the playroom, convinced that the therapist wants to harm them. Sometimes, repetition also happens within the play, for example, when the child asks the therapist to play out that they abandon the child somewhere. In this way, all kinds of feelings, powerful anxieties and overwhelming events can be shown gradually and sometimes indirectly in play, before being mastered step by step and via many detours. This therapeutic repetition helps to communicate in a safe context about difficult experiences and to regain control of the trauma experienced as well as of the self-experience. It comes down to mastery and regaining control of one's own story. In therapy literature, we call this re-enactment. The child controls the interaction with the therapist in such a way that the level of arousal and stress during the re-enactment can remain bearable. Play therefore offers a child a safe place, a space in which they can experiment as they like and can tolerate, without being hindered by the rules and demands of physical and social reality (Lieberman et al., 2015, pp. 100–101). The child can reverse the roles, and as a child, yell at the adult therapist, if that fits within the roles of the angry teacher who flies off the handle against a child because they made a mistake. Or the child can make the adult repeat a nasty experience, by letting the therapist play out that they are a terrible doctor who hurts and abuses the child. The child can influence the course of the play, and in the next play session, change the story's ending.

Psychotherapy: a joint venture to find language and images for experiences

Meaning-making happens through metaphors (Bleyen, 2012, p. 155). When we incorporate a traumatic experience into our life story, meaning is created by, among other things, presenting the elusive trauma as something else, in an understandable image or story. Helping children to find precisely these metaphors or images that fit in with what they have experienced is therefore a powerful and important aspect of processing and giving meaning. For example, Maya recognises herself immediately in a song by Bart Peeters: 'Allemaal door jou' ('All because of you'), a metaphor for how 'everything I do wrong is your fault, because you left me' (see Chapter 7).

Through play scenes, stories, fantasy play and drawings, the child's flexibility of thinking, processing and mentalizing is enhanced. New twists and turns emerge, new fantasies that support the processing and increase coping, new images of oneself and others. Throughout the therapy sessions, the child's communication will also change. The game 'I was the boss and you were the naughty child' means that the child can imagine something else than what has previously happened. 'I can imagine that I am the boss of what is happening' is often one of the first transformations in therapy: from powerlessness and helplessness to having a handle on and control over what is happening. Although this is far from being the end of processing, it shows that a new sense of self is developing, a self that can act in difficult circumstances – something the child could not do at the time of the trauma. The new sense of self is a basis from which further processing can become possible.

This change also helps the child to disassociate themselves from the trauma. The child is no longer only equated to 'the abused child', the victim. There is a growing distance between the self and the traumatic experience: 'I am not a horrible child, but horrible things have been done to me', or 'I have been abandoned, but not because I am worthless'. To facilitate these shifts in self-image or self-experience, drawing and playing are essential in child psychotherapy. Drawing can sometimes give a very concrete image of an experience; play offers the possibility to convey through all kinds of re-enactments what is going on in the child's thinking process and feelings. Through these images from drawings and play, we help a child to understand themselves better, to discover new – or sometimes also old – pieces of themselves, and then to find starting points for new behavioural and relationship patterns. As therapists, we sometimes see that a child reveals a fragment of a traumatic experience; it is only in a later phase of treatment that it becomes possible for a more comprehensive narrative or representation of that experience to take shape. In the subsequent therapy phase, images and metaphors can lead to new, more helpful images of oneself and others. We sometimes see how, at a given moment, a child learns to think something that was previously unthinkable (see also Chapter 8).

Concluding thought

Where these children tend to keep others at a distance or re-enact traumatising relational experiences, often accompanied by unreachable or difficult behaviour towards their new caregiving figures, therapy can first of all help them to express inner emptiness, chaos or threat. This is revealed in fragments, sometimes with various detours, so that the therapist has to be receptive towards these fragments of expression and search for meaning with the child. This search is always with a lot of trial and error, breakdowns in play, and relapse. This is only possible with the therapist as a reliable witness, who makes the sometimes very disorganised and disrupted communication of the traumatised child important, and makes room for further searching for meaning within a predictable frame. This is crucial as 'delightfully and inescapably, we have storytelling brains' (Roberts, 1999, p. 7).

6 From emotional rollercoaster to controllable vehicle

DOI: 10.4324/9781003155645-9

A rapidly dysregulated inner world

Regulation is about how a child learns to recognise, accept and tolerate, understand and manage themselves, their sensations and physical signals. This lays the building blocks for how the child will later be able to endure feelings, and will be able to use them to understand and solve situations, and to process difficult experiences. It is also about the meanings that these sensations and signals can acquire in the course of one's life. For example, is a feeling of boredom something one can let be for a while, or that one even needs as a breeding ground for a creative impulse; or does a feeling of boredom lead instead to a moment of panic because one is in danger of sinking into the void, and will then do anything to avoid that situation? Some children can tolerate tumult, strife and tension better than deep boredom and emptiness, which will make them do something – at the most unpredictable moments – that is guaranteed to cause tumult.

> *At the calmest family moments, Ophelia suddenly does all kinds of things to annoy her older brother, thereby spoiling every pleasant family moment. First, she winds her brother up, then the other children start to misbehave and finally her parents get angry, because she makes family moments, which are so important to them, impossible.*

Negative and potentially overwhelming experiences are part of any child's development (see Chapter 2). In a young child, stress – due to hunger, cold, boredom, overstimulation – is initially regulated by the parent, who keeps an eye on things like a 'monitor' when the baby becomes upset and needs redirecting. The parent gets to know their child through close observation: 'I'd better tuck her in tightly, that will help her to settle', 'When she screams so loudly, it's better to wait a bit before giving her a bottle, until she is a little soothed, otherwise she will just throw it back up straight away', and so on. So, the first regulation is a regulation to which the caregiving figure makes a major contribution and is therefore referred to as 'co-regulation'. As a child grows up, moments in which they are able to regulate themselves alternate with moments in which they need the caregiving figure. The parent 'monitors' less and less and gradually gives the child more space to regulate themselves, to master their anxieties themselves ('Stay in bed, you can do it') or to regain balance after mild distress ('Let him look on with his sad face, he'll join in the game again in a moment'). In other words, 'self-regulation' gradually takes over from co-regulation.

Children who have experienced complex trauma often struggle long and intensely with regulation issues, as 'following a history of early deprivation, even mild stress later in life can elicit severe reactivity and dysfunction' (Cook et al., 2003, p. 10). They often do not know what to do with their emotions and feel they are at the mercy of intense emotional swings. Their inner world is like an unpredictable emotional 'rollercoaster'; their emotional temperature quickly switches from freezing point to boiling point and back again. With such a complex inner world, it is very difficult for a child to keep a cool head and behave like a calm and thoughtful individual who can accurately describe what is going on or ask for what they need. This makes the child very unpredictable for their environment. Children who have experienced complex trauma have to rely on co-regulation for much longer than caregiving figures expect, based on their experiences with children on a more optimal developmental path. It is not enough for the child that someone listens to them for a moment, or offers comforting words; what is needed are parents who take over regulation much longer and more frequently.

Below, we explain how we (1) understand this emotional rollercoaster, (2) help a child in psychotherapy to recognise, experience, tolerate and regulate stress signals, sensations and emotions and (3) help find meaning so that the intense emotions can be absorbed into a meaningful narrative. Arousal and affect are, after all, important themes in the psychotherapeutic process of a child who has experienced complex trauma.

Traumatised children often think of themselves as 'mad' or 'naughty', because their behaviour cannot always be rationally explained, because the intensity of their reactions – in the eyes of others – is not always in proportion to the trigger, because their actions are not always appropriate for the context or because their difficult attempts at communication cause anger or disappointment in others. Experiences and fantasies are gradually 'normalised' by a reliable, safe and sensitive therapist, who helps the child experience that their difficult-to-read and clumsy attempts at communication are important. This 'normalisation' of reactions as inherent to the processing of traumatic experiences (Lieberman et al., 2015) is crucial for the child attempting to acquire new capacities in regulating and relating.

Figure 6.1 Traumatised children's kettle boiling over.

Hypervigilance and increased sensitivity to stress: the biopsychosocial trap

While his adoptive parents tell their story during a first intake meeting, James engages in play with knights preparing for an attack on their castle. When the therapist asks where the attack will come from, he answers that no one knows. It might come down from the sky or from over land!

Raphael's mother relates how it sometimes seems as if Raphael has completely forgotten what he learned a week earlier. It is as though he has never heard of it, that it is just completely unknown. As such, he is not developing at the same pace as his peers. It seems as though absorbing new knowledge is becoming more and more difficult for him.

The fact that the affective balance of traumatised children is disrupted so quickly, and dysregulation is never far away, has everything to do with early life experiences that have made their stress system hypersensitive. Disconcerting and overwhelming experiences in the early years of life, which had an unbearable intensity for the child, caused overpowering and threatening anxieties. To prevent the child from ever experiencing this threat again, the brain has developed in such a way that the child is prepared for it. Regulation of sensations, stress signals and affect is then affected in three ways by complex trauma. Growing up in an unpredictable environment has led to (1) a perceptual hypervigilance to be prepared for the worst or 'eyes and ears that are constantly scanning the environment for danger', (2) a physical hypersensitivity to fear or a body that has to be ready at all times to respond to an unexpected intrusive experience, leading to fight, flight or freeze behaviour and (3) a normal, mild signal anxiety[1] that has given way to a generalised and permanent powerful sense of anxiety that overshadows affective life. This alertness to danger that was once necessary and adaptive not only becomes superfluous in the changed circumstances of, for example, a new family, but it often turns out that it has taken on a life of its own. A child with an over-active stress system continues to scan the situation around them for threat or danger. It is this experience that James expresses in his play described above: 'Your system is hypervigilant, you have to be constantly prepared for an attack, and you never know from which angle that attack will come'.

This state of continuous hyperarousal and excessive anxiety that can lead to emotional outbursts then triggers a flood of other potential problems.

1 It undermines the ability to learn because it is impossible for a child to concentrate for long periods of time on anything other than scanning danger. In order to learn new things, one must be able to find sufficient calmness. As long as a child needs to invest all energy in surviving the continuous (threat of) dysregulation, there is little room for learning and growth processes. Going through life hypervigilantly and anxiously often goes hand in hand with attention problems in the classroom.

2 Increased alertness makes the child switch to an aggressive mode more quickly. Always on the lookout for signs of potential danger, they easily 'overreact' and generalise, which triggers the outbursts of anger for which these children are often referred. At the slightest sign of – real or perceived – danger, the reaction is triggered at full scale, without nuance. Frustrations which for an observer seem relatively 'minor' can signify great danger from the child's perspective, and lead to 'overly' aggressive reactions.

3 All this hampers relationships with others. The outbursts of anger strain relationships. With a child who is reasonable and pleasant one moment, and kicks and hits violently the next, it is much more difficult to maintain a positive and warm bond, and not to fall

back into volatile communication. For parents, siblings and teachers, as well as friends, trainers and coaches in sports or other hobbies, this requires that they know how to deal sensitively with the intense regulation difficulties that a traumatised child confronts them with. The hypervigilant 'scanning' and suspicious attitude can cause caregiving figures to feel uncomfortably controlled or watched, or 'spied on', as one foster mother called it.

4 The uncontrolled temper tantrums often have a serious impact on the development of the child's sense of self and self-image. Afterwards, children are sometimes overwhelmed by unbearable feelings of shame and guilt, which in turn create an additional upset in the already turbulent emotional inner world. After all, this intense shame and guilt sometimes prevent them from admitting – to themselves and to others – that they have done something that was not acceptable, which of course is the basis for making amends.

5 Later developmental tasks and affective demands – such as engaging in and maintaining friendships (socialisation) and learning new things, such as in hobbies (exploration) at elementary school age, or dealing with emergent sexuality as an adolescent – lead to a new tangle of inextricable feelings. So, not only can a child's early developments be difficult, but later developments are also not always free from problems. That is why we sometimes refer to the 'biopsychosocial trap' (Shalev, 2000) in which children who have experienced complex trauma can get stuck. The biologically anchored hyperarousal leads to psychological and social difficulties, which in turn cause more anxiety, hyperarousal and stress. The vicious cycle is then complete.

The continuum of arousal in traumatised children

> *Mum treats both her daughters to ice cream in the park. When a dog suddenly gets too close, Mum is alarmed and shouts at it. Beatrice looks up, but keeps licking her ice cream. Yet, Christine has been startled by her mother's fearful reaction. She drops her ice cream and starts crying. It takes her two full hours to calm down again.*

A sequence of being alerted and calming down again in frightening situations is part of everyday life for any child. It is just about the most important developmental task a child has to grapple with during the first three months of life: being able to be calm, alert and interested in moments when negative arousal from hunger, cold and fatigue, for example, disappear into the background for a while. Everyone is familiar with experiences ranging from a moment of panic in mild situations (a computer crashing at the wrong moment) to serious situations (a child having an accident), after which the stress system in the brain becomes deactivated again and a state of calm returns as soon as an experience is recognised as familiar or resolved, and/or assessed as safe (Perry & Szalavitz, 2006, p. 48). When all the data from your computer can still be salvaged, or the damage from the accident does not prove to be life-threatening, you gradually calm down again. Only in a situation of relative calm can a person concentrate, for example, on a book, (school) work, a conversation or something they are doing in the here and now. Only in a situation of relative calm – an optimal level of activation or arousal – can a person think and talk about something, can they concentrate and learn. Only with relative calm can a person control themselves and their actions and make use of the higher (regulatory and cognitive) capacities of the brain, such as the ability to reason abstractly, reflect on motives and backgrounds (mentalizing), make plans, dream about the future, etc.

> *If you are in the library reading and someone drops a heavy book on a table, the loud noise will immediately make you stop reading. You will activate your arousal response, focus on the source of the noise, categorise it as a safe, familiar accident – perhaps annoying but nothing to worry about. If, on the other hand, you hear a loud noise in the library, turn and discover that other people around you seem alarmed, then look up and see a man with a gun, your brain would move from arousal to alarm and probably then into full-blown fear. If in a few minutes, you learn that this was a bad student prank, your brain would slowly move back down this arousal continuum toward a state of calm.*
>
> ***Perry & Szalavitz (2006, p. 48)***

During the course of the day, every child's level of arousal fluctuates across a continuum (see Table 6.1) according to the new experiences they have (Perry & Szalavitz, 2006). When confronted with a new situation or new information, the brain starts to assess the situation

Table 6.1 Arousal continuum (Based on Perry & Szalavitz, 2006)

Internal state	Calm	Alert	Alarm	Fear	Terror
Arousal continuum	Rest	Vigilance	Resistance Crying	Defiance Tantrums	Fight, flight or freeze
Sense of time	Future	Days Hours	Hours Minutes	Minutes Seconds	No sense of time
Cognitive style	Abstract	Concrete	Emotional	Reactive	Reflexive

(appraisal) and assess whether or not it is dangerous (evaluation). The child then becomes more alert, the thinking style becomes more concrete and more focused on the current situation. This is comparable to how an adult can feel in a new situation or a foreign airport when travelling alone, not knowing where to go or whom to ask for information. Even if one has a lot of time to read a book, they don't really dive deep into the story, they stay alert for small movements around them. One is then automatically less focused on more abstract contents or contents at a greater distance, such as the history or maths class. As anxiety increases, thinking and reacting becomes more primitive and the sense of time becomes more narrow.

The brain and stress system of children who have experienced complex trauma have developed in such a way that they switch faster from calm to extremely anxious and panic-stricken, as though there were no gradations. 'Minor anxieties', such as signal anxiety, for example, do not exist, so that the threshold above which anxiety and panic are experienced is much lower. It is all or nothing, as though there is only an 'on and off' switch. Indeed, the life-saving anxiety that switches off nuanced thinking in each of us in life-threatening situations enables faster reactions, which help us to survive. However, this high anxiety becomes maladaptive when it persists and is generalised into a continuous state of heightened arousal, even in a calmer environment. In the course of a seemingly 'stressless' school day, children who have experienced complex trauma move across the arousal continuum from calm to inner panic. This switch is reached quickly and suddenly. There is no gradual build-up of stress, so those around them often don't see it coming: a minor increase in stress immediately leads to an overwhelming reaction.

This process explains part of their unpredictable and unaccountable behaviour on the playground or in the school bus: 'I raised my fist, because he gave me such a nasty look!' or 'I tried to throw open the door of the car when we were driving home, because she (mother) didn't want me anymore. I heard what she said, you know!' On top of that, a hypervigilant system also takes a lot more effort and time to calm down again.

> *As the eldest child, Christine had been involved in the long and intense conflictual family situation. Her sister Beatrice had managed to withdraw herself more when things kicked off at home. Although both sisters are doing fairly well now, Christine in particular remains extremely stress-sensitive, finding it very difficult to calm down after an intensely disruptive event. After being startled for a moment by her mother's – hypervigilant – reaction, she cannot be reassured quickly, but instead the arousal keeps simmering in her body for hours.*

Trauma triggers

What was covered above means that a child who has experienced complex trauma has an inner world that is not very predictable for either themselves or their environment. Intense emotions can suddenly overwhelm them because they hear, smell, think or dream something; because unexpected experiences trigger something in their system that they have little control over. These unexpected experiences are referred to as 'trauma triggers'. Something has set the child's system to hypervigilant, and often they themselves don't know precisely what it was. As humans, we are equipped with memory mechanisms like these trauma triggers, which are designed to protect us from a traumatic event being repeated.

> *Peter, having escaped a fire, experiences how the smell of fire suddenly catapults him back to the moment when the fire started in his kitchen. He experiences the same sensations that he went through when he was in the middle of a burning kitchen. Veronica feels nauseous from anxiety and panic at the sound of splashing water, ever since she survived a tsunami years ago. Tara suddenly starts to tremble heavily every time the phone rings. It all started with the phone call she got from her father when he told her that her mother had died.*

When the anxiety at the smell of fire, the sound of sloshing water or the ring of the telephone reminds a person of a traumatic experience, they will try to escape from the recurrence of that nasty experience. This alert mechanism helps us to survive by recognising threatening situations. The same mechanism, however, turns against us when it begins to lead a life of its own; when it continues to evoke the pain and anxiety of the original moment at any sensory impulse that resembles the traumatic event in any way. Seemingly 'normal' experiences such as a smell, a sound, a movement, a facial expression, etc. then become 'trauma triggers' that put a child in a state of heightened anxiety or vigilance. For example, a baby that has often heard arguing adults yell at each other may recoil at a loud voice in the new (foster or adoptive) family. This can confuse the foster carers or adoptive parents, who do not always understand why a child can be calmly occupied one moment but suddenly becomes intensely anxious or extremely angry the next. After all, the parents do not consider their differences of opinion that they express with mild intensity as serious or disruptive, and therefore do not understand why such an innocent incident evokes such an intense reaction in their child.

What makes it even more difficult for the outside world is that internal stimuli, such as hunger and a feeling of loss or deprivation, can also act as trauma triggers. For some adopted children, for example, there is no such thing as 'a little hunger': every hunger stimulus is a trauma trigger, eliciting the experience that the feeling of hunger takes over all control from them. It is as though unstoppable forces from their painful empty stomach are attacking their body. This experience pumps the adrenaline through their body and leads to the feeling that they might 'go mad with hunger'. Naturally, the child doesn't then react by calmly asking for a sandwich or biscuit, but they go crazy, screaming and shouting at anyone in their path. They grab their food, disregarding the rules of politeness that apply in a context where there is enough food. Even though there is no shortage in their new life circumstances, the reaction to a simple hunger stimulus is driven by deep memories of deprivation and unbearable hunger.

As a result, trauma triggers not only lead to anxiety within the child, but also to intense stress reactions and then to behaviours meant to reduce this stress: 'I flew at my brother's throat because he looked at me in that way! He was really going to hurt me'. Although this behaviour is understandable within the original traumatic context, it often forms a stream of 'false' constructions when circumstances have changed (the brother may have wanted to challenge – as brothers do – but not really hurt). And this, in turn, can seriously strain the new relationships.

First aid in case of dysregulation: co-regulating adults who breathe deeply and think calmly

Precisely because regulation problems weigh so heavily on all other areas of development, they always take precedence over the other themes we work on with children who have experienced complex trauma. Perry (2017) says: 'Regulate, then relate, then reason'. When regulation issues arise, they must be dealt with first. Regulation always takes precedence because it is only on the basis of (re)finding a minimal level of calmness and regulation that we can start work on relational issues, or we can discuss and think together about what is going on in the person's life.

A hypervigilant child who is intensely anxious is, first and foremost, in need of an adult who can help them calm down. Such co-regulation requires a caregiving figure who, in a moment of complete dysregulation, manages to remain 'older, wiser and more sensible'; who does not panic or go into heightened arousal; who does not react in a belittling or sadistic way; who perceptibly and persistently continues to help the child to calm down again; and who knows how to 'cool things down in the heat of the moment'. Talking about what happened, looking for solutions, thinking of possibilities for repair, a structuring intervention or a punishment: this is all for the next phase, when the stress level has dropped back to bearable proportions. Traumatised children's level and intensity of dysregulation initially require a different approach from parents or educators, than the usual enquiring as to the reason for the child's behaviour. Any question in a state of heightened stress will only result in more arguing or more stress and arousal in the child, and/or in new conflicts. Helping the child recognise that they are upset (how it is) is much more crucial here than asking what is going on (why it is like this).

However, being able to remain calm themselves requires extraordinary reflectivity and stress regulation from parents. In order to be able to help the child, a caregiving figure must first be able to calm themselves down and keep a cool head, above and beyond the disappointment that the child is once again displaying difficult behaviour, above and beyond the fear that they will do really stupid things and above and beyond their anger that boundaries have been roundly crossed. In this respect, children who have experienced complex trauma require extraordinary caregiving figures, who are not only able to remain calm and find room to reflect again and again, but who are also willing to tolerate the stress and anxiety that is inevitably 'done to' them. A child who experiences a lot of anxiety and stress inevitably also risks 'infecting' their environment with a lot of anxiety and stress. In interacting with this child during very stressful moments, the caregiving figures themselves are generally also given a 'stress shower': an immersion in the stress into which the child – as is often the case – has been thrust at that moment. This 'shower' often has a toxic effect on the child's environment: it is a painful and threatening surge of stress, which the caregiving figure experiences at first-hand and which can leave even balanced caregiving figures badly affected and unbalanced. These children project the stress they experience to the outside world and, of course, set the stress in motion there. Stress and tension that arise in a traumatised child are similar to what happens when a pebble is thrown into a pond. The stress is first and foremost situated in the feeling and thinking of the child (the circle where the pebble hits the water), but is then inevitably also felt in those around them (the rippling circles in the water).

Figure 6.2 First aid in case of dysregulation.

Images, words and language as a basis for regulation and control

Only after the 'first aid' has been given – that is, the support to regain calmness and regulation – does talking about what happened gain importance. As long as any arousal or emotion leads to a crescendo – any (seemingly) 'minor' moment of negativity or anger leads to almost uncontrollable explosiveness – the children (and their parents) experience this difficult-to-regulate and emotionally overwhelming inner world as something that runs on uncontrollably; as a 'lack of built-in brakes'.

> *He tries so hard to get those brakes into his system, but they're not his brakes.*
>
> LUKE'S MUM

In such cases, emerging regulation is about experiencing a – sometimes very nascent – sense of control over physical and psychological processes. It's about the feeling that one can sit in the driving seat oneself and handle the powerful engine of one's car, without being constantly controlled by what's going on inside one's body.

Words can be helpful in this regard. In order to clarify how, in psychotherapy, we look for words and language to express arousal, affect and emotion, we now make a small side step to 'normal' development. A baby gets to know its emotional world with the help of adult caregiving figures who, among other things, provide words for experiences. This helps children to understand themselves and the world around them. The sequence of sounds 'mummyscoming' gradually begins to sound reassuring when the carer at day care utters similar words in a comforting way; or when daddy says with a funny voice 'ickle pain', the child understands that daddy means 'slightly hurt' – something the child clearly felt just before. When, as a toddler, you kick the table leg you just ran into, grandpa asks: 'Are you angry at the table, did it hurt you?' And when you bite your brother's hand because he took your puzzle away, grandma says you might well be angry with your brother, but you mustn't bite him.

When a child is not provided with words for what is going on in their inner world, they miss out on the necessary tools to understand and further differentiate their inner world. Without words to describe differentiated feelings, one's emotional world remains a taxing and possibly meaningless or even 'crazy' or 'disturbed' jumble, which one would rather push to the background.

> *'Annoying' is the word that L has used for quite a while for everything he experiences as negative inside. He can recognise that when he feels 'annoyed', it makes his parents and brothers angry. But understanding why he finds something 'annoying' and knowing whether this 'annoying' feeling is a feeling of anger, sadness or loneliness is far too difficult for him, and will be for a long time to come. In the same way, it has long been an impossible task for Laura to give words to that indefinable 'irritating' feeling she struggles with internally. As a result, she has no other way but to get rid of it physically: toys are thrown around the therapy room, furniture is pushed over, Laura crawls across the floor of the playroom and laughs uncontrollably. With the therapist's support, some kind of thinking and talking process can gradually emerge as to 'whether it could be that her body is showing that her mind is in a state of extreme discomfort and chaos'. Thinking about what exactly could be the cause of this discomfort and chaos will not be on the horizon for a long time. Much later in therapy, Laura brings a 'feelings thermometer' to the session, which she received from the foster care worker a year earlier and which she has since supplemented with feeling words. She asks the therapist what these words all mean.*

About 'being inside' or 'outside your window': metaphors to help children understand themselves

In order to provide children in psychotherapy with words for how an inner world can get disrupted quickly and violently following a traumatic experience, Ogden and colleagues (2000, 2006, 2015) developed the metaphor of the 'window of tolerance'. This metaphor helps both children and parents to think about what is going on internally in terms of the arousal and affect continuum that we explained earlier.

This 'window' or 'frame' refers to the level of arousal and affect that a person can tolerate and finds optimal. There is an 'optimal zone' of arousal and affect within which a person feels comfortable. This zone presupposes a certain degree of emotional calm within which activity can occur. We often present this 'zone' to children as the 'green zone' in which it is pleasant to be. Only within this zone of optimal arousal can one be attentive in class, learn something new, be focused on something, read a book, have a conversation and

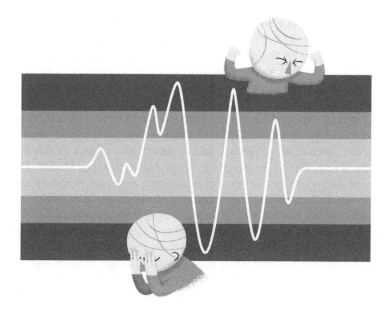

Figure 6.3 The window of tolerance.

enjoy the pleasant excitement in the run-up to Christmas. As long as one's emotions are characterised by the manageable ups and downs of ordinary life, a person can be who they are, stay relaxed at work, enjoy what is going on around them, enjoy sports, have a discussion with their teacher or their partner without this getting out of hand. Within this zone of arousal and affect, a person's thinking remains sufficiently 'online' to shape their daily life in an ordinary way. Within this zone of arousal and affect, a person's 'human brain' is doing its work.

However, when there is too much sensation, stress or affect, a person becomes anxious, angry or upset, and this emotion is more likely to be overwhelming. The person enters the 'red zone', and their whole system has just one focus: 'How do I get rid of this excess emotion?' They react angrily, agitatedly and irritatedly. Because this excess of arousal and affect elicits the person to react like a wild lion that is backed into a corner, it seems like their 'mammal brain' momentarily takes over. Throughout one's life and within one's specific environment, a person has developed their own personal ways to get rid of these overly intense and unpleasant feelings, to get out of this 'red zone' again. One child finds peace by going to available others to whom they can tell their story, or from whom they expect an affectionate word or a hug, while another child finds peace by withdrawing into their shell and doing something on their own, with music for example or by playing sports.

A lack of sensation, stress or affect can also be a serious problem. For some children, for example, feeling bored is intolerable, because it puts them in a deep state of emptiness. When boredom strikes, these children feel apathetic, lethargic and inside their own prison, ending up in the 'blue zone' of tedium and despondency, of lack of life and vitality. They then go in search of things that activate, stimulate and energise them, so that they do not completely sink into boredom and apathy. In such cases, it is as though the 'reptile brain' is at work.

People differ significantly in terms of how large the window of optimally tolerable affect is for them. For example, one person loves watching thrillers, without falling prey to hyperarousal, while another finds the tension so unbearable that they can't sleep, even though it's only a film. Likewise, one person likes physically intense challenges, and high and fast experiences, while the other gets nauseous just at the thought of them.

In children who have experienced complex trauma, regulation is impaired, causing them to 'leap' from one zone to another more quickly; from 'ordinary' intense to overwhelming experience for example, or from 'ordinary' intense experience to boredom and inner emptiness. Moreover, their optimal zone of what is pleasant and bearable affect is much more narrow, their margin is much smaller. This explains why these children are not only upset by negative emotions, such as when they are angry or scared, but also by an increasing intensity of positive feelings, such as the excitement associated with a birthday party, or of looking forward to Christmas or a fieldtrip with the class. It can already be very helpful for the child to get to know themselves in this respect, so that they can learn to protect themselves from excessive exposure to situations that disrupt their regulation. It may be important for the family to realise that it will not be possible, for quite some time, to take the child along to amusement parks or parties where they will have to endure a lot of stimuli – too much stimuli to be able to tolerate.

In psychotherapy, children who have experienced complex trauma often quickly recognise and understand how they suddenly go into 'the red zone' or feel their 'mammal brain' (Ogden & Fisher, 2015) leaping into action when they experience increased anxiety or stress.

For Maya, 'boredom' is often the reason to start playing video games. Moments of boredom are so difficult for her that she simply reaches for the tablet and starts gaming. Gaming makes her feel alive and vital. After all, these games have a lot of exciting and fun things going on. The trap Maya often falls into is that she can't stop, because the moment the game stops, she is immediately catapulted back into the void, which is so hard to bear. Not being able to get away from her gaming, in turn, causes new problems. So, Maya's attempts to get out of the deep boredom ('blue zone') regularly cause her to end up in hyperarousal ('red zone'). She frequently gets into serious conflict with her parents. Or, she loses sight of the fact that she has to get dressed and get ready to play sports with friends. When they are at the door, she is then so deeply embarrassed that she doesn't dare to open the door, leaving her friends to go off by themselves. When her mother comes home a little while later, it is obvious how intensely the emotion has built up in the meantime. Maya then takes the whole thing out on her mother, staying in a raging temper all afternoon.

About lions, deer and rabbits: falling prey to primitive fight, flight or freeze modes

As child therapists, we would like to add a few more animal metaphors, to help children understand what primitive mechanisms such as fight, flight and freeze do to them when they are stressed. At moments of extremely high anxiety, prompted by a traumatic experience or by a subsequent trauma trigger, fight or flight are the primitive mechanisms that do their work as an automatic reaction beyond a person's control. These mechanisms come to the child's aid uninvited at times of stress – whatever the source of the stress. The human nervous system is, after all, the result of the flight or fight reaction of an animal that is in danger (Turnbull, 2012). The human brain is, therefore, first and foremost, a 'survival organ' that keep us at a distance from danger, and only in the second instance also a 'thinking organ'. In threatening situations, our central nervous system comes into action, transforming us – in a fast and instinctive process – to 'another version of ourselves'. In a 'normal state', we can focus our attention on normal, day-to-day things, but in a life-threatening emergency situation, we can only do two things: flee from the threat (flight) or face it (fight). In

Figure 6.4 Dysregulation as a 'bomb' shutting down traumatised children's 'thinking brain'.

the milliseconds that we need to get into a state of fight or flight, neurotransmitters and hormones fire into action to bring about enormous changes in our bodies.

A child who flies into fight mode goes straight on the attack. They get angry, shout and scream or even start lashing out because they feel frightened and threatened.

In the school bus, L has screamed at a teacher because he felt he had been treated unfairly. In therapy, he recognises straight away that in the playground, he reacts 'like an angry lion', like the time he lashed out – before thinking about it – when someone shouted a racist remark at his best friend. When talking about this in therapy, L is well aware that this is not the best solution, and can easily think of different and better ways to react at such moments. With the therapist, he thinks about how he could recognise something starting to happen in his body, and how he could do something other than lashing out with his fists. In consultation with the school, 'time-out areas' are established, where L can go when he feels the fight impulse coming: some teachers and the headmaster are willing to be available as confidants to give him a place to cool off immediately, to prevent him from 'getting outside of his window', until he is able to control himself and apply the brakes in such situations.

In addition to the image of the lion, children also recognise how, in the same state of feeling overwhelmed, they may react like a deer: gripped by anxiety, anger and chaos, they flee and run off (flight). A 'flight mode' is the rash and reflexive tendency to run away from the source of stress. Some children jump on their bikes and ride around to calm down, or – what is more problematic – run away from home without saying where they are going, because they can't cope with the conflict with mum or dad for the moment.

> *Maya hurt herself at the fair. As she couldn't grasp fast enough that dad wanted to help and comfort her, she ran off anxious, disappointed and angry.*

Similarly, lying or pretending they know of nothing when the child has been up to something can also be regarded as flight behaviour.

Aside from fight and flight, 'freeze mode' is the most primitive way of reacting to stress and anxiety. The child stiffens up like a rabbit caught in headlights, as though they are 'not there' internally, and 'freezes', as it were, in a withdrawn and unreachable state. They stare blankly and shut off all senses, to prevent stressful messages from coming in. This state is also called 'dissociation' and goes hand in hand with losing touch with the external environment and with the internal subjective experience (Schmeets, 2005). Sometimes, the child barely remembers what exactly happened afterwards and seems to have to 'land back' in their body and environment; the unbearable affect is not shared with others. The child has withdrawn from the world and has to be brought back to it. Dissociation is also noticeable in young children. They turn away, often turning their gaze to a fixed point and repeating certain behaviours (Benoit, 2010). In a dissociated state, the affect is split off and no longer experienced (Perry et al., 1995). However, this regulatory mechanism is very harmful to psychological development. It leads to parts of psychological functioning no longer being accessible to conscious life. The individual will no longer be able to mentalize these events later in life (Schmeets, 2011, p. 41).

Fight, flight and freeze modes of children who have experienced complex trauma require a lot from the parents' resources and reflective capabilities. Seeing one's child hitting someone in public, suddenly running away at a family party or in an amusement park, or seeing how they can suddenly become completely unreachable, are experiences that deeply affect and sometimes dysregulate parents.

Regaining trust in one's own body

Traumatic experiences are stored in the body. They drain the body's agility and fluidity because the body can only defend itself against trauma by becoming silent, numb, sick or tense. In this sense, the body carries the signs of something one does not like to return to – an experience that is hurtful and traumatic. After all, the body is the seat of emotional life: it is where we feel tension, or peace and contentment, where we experience anger, but equally intense happiness. The physical feeling requires to be captured in images and words. Without this further processing in the form of images and words, the body remains in a place where stress prevails following a traumatic experience, and which shows what is going on through symptoms, or conversely, which becomes completely numb so as not to be overwhelmed by trauma again.

A calmer environment and a therapeutic space afford the opportunity to get closer to the trauma encapsulated in the body, and to 'liberate' the body that has become a carrier of an unprocessed element. To this end, these experiences that have been stored in the body as vague sensations need to be 'experienced and imagined', 'drawn, played out and put into words' on a psychological level. In psychotherapy with children who have experienced complex trauma, this means, first and foremost, to help the child to learn to take their body seriously again, and to learn to 'read' body signals: let what is happening happen and use that as information about what is going on, in and around oneself.

> *On her way to the playroom, Laura – who was seriously neglected in her early years – tells the therapist that her teacher, who gave birth a while ago, will visit school tomorrow with her baby. The conversation immediately evokes in Laura an image of 'not having been breastfed, because she was born prematurely and Mummy did not have enough milk for her', as well as the difficult feelings of fundamental lack that go with it. Later in the session, it turns out that earlier that day Laura had felt completely lost at school, trying to find the room where gym class had been moved to, and got a nasty graze on her belly. While telling all this, Laura had sat down on the table with her feet resting on a chair. It doesn't take long before she kicks the chair over. Laura says: 'I didn't want to do it, the chair wanted it', and starts laughing uncontrollably.*

'Stop and rewind': from fight, flight and freeze to playing, talking and thinking together

The consistently held premise that all behaviour originates from a dynamic inner world of thoughts, wishes, anxieties, etc., affords an important opportunity for change in therapy. It helps children to lay the first foundations to be less concerned with survival and their own fragile equilibrium. This approach makes them more accessible and more social. Their experiences become more meaningful and can become part of a different story about themselves in relation to others. Discontinuous and incoherent experiences make way for continuity in the self-experience: threads and fragments of experiences become interwoven into a new and more coherent self-narrative.

As adult caregivers and educators, we try to attune to what is happening in these children's present reality, and from there, we look for aspects of their inner world – alert to vague emotions and impressions, and to elements that appear in a drawing but cannot yet be put into words. In this way, we help them to give meaning to multiple experiences in which they are at the mercy of overwhelming inner forces.

Cara is seven years old and constantly having minor accidents, in which she 'suddenly' seems to be in a situation without understanding what is happening or how to deal with it. Her only solution is to deny that something is going on: no matter how obvious it is to everyone else that she has 'messed up' something, she insists that she knows nothing about it. Parents call this flight behaviour 'lying'. From a parental perspective, this is, of course, a logical conclusion. However, children can only lie once they are able to grasp an experience in language and then knowingly and intentionally twist it or withhold it. From the outside, denial looks like lying, but in a child's inner world, it is a more raw and primitive process, which in essence is more similar to the flight reaction: the child resolves something they find too difficult by pretending it doesn't exist, and they persist in doing so until finally, they actually believe it themselves.

In a therapy session together with Cara, her mother tells the therapist about an incident in the bathroom. Mother found the sink full of nail polish stains. She suspected that Cara wanted to experiment with mother's nail polish and had an accident. Cara continues to deny this for the next few days. Mum explains how, as parents, they feel powerless and angry, and how they are unable to talk to Cara about such an 'innocent' incident. In order to help her get in touch with what might be going on inside her, the therapist starts offering language, almost in a similar way to how one offers language to a much younger child when seeing that they are going through a difficult experience. Thinking aloud, like when telling a story, the therapist begins to explain that children often have good reason to say that they haven't done something, and that she can think of some examples. The therapist says, 'It's possible that a child just didn't do something ...' Even though she doesn't believe in that scenario herself, she presents it as a possibility, so as to take Cara along in a process of thinking-together-about. The therapist continues: 'It may also be that a child sometimes says "I didn't do it", because they really have no idea how to handle and resolve a problem like this, or because they are afraid of how angry or disappointed mum and dad might be...' Cara has been nodding her head in agreement since the therapist has been talking. Her mother relaxes visibly and looks relieved. An initial moment of understanding and connection between mother and Cara emerges. When Cara is invited to draw what exactly happened, she draws the sink, full of stains of nail polish. A 'scene' is set up, an image is sketched.

In order to get more than just a scene, but also facilitate a 'story' (or narrative) in which the characters who act, think and feel get a place, the therapist asks whether Cara also wants to draw herself

Figure 6.5 Cara's drawing.

into it. Cara draws a girl looking at the stains in the sink, with her hands covering her face.

Her mother immediately joins in, suddenly discovering something significant and meaningful in the drawing. She says: 'But Cara, were you scared yourself perhaps?' Again, Cara nods in agreement and approaches her mother, who puts her arm around her. Suddenly Cara's behaviour is no longer 'strange', 'naughty' or 'disturbed' to her mother; it takes on significance and meaning from her daughter's emotional world. 'She's lying' is replaced with 'She was so frightened herself, and she doesn't know how to handle that feeling'. The conversation then continues about how you might also ask for help when you have done something you don't know what to do about. It's about how you might be afraid that your mum or dad might be angry or disappointed, and how you can find solutions together. Ideas come up, such as a note under mum's or dad's pillow; putting a notepad somewhere in the house, in which you can write about these things, to share them with each other; or how you can leave each other a sign that you want to communicate something that you can't yet say or write down in pictures or words.

Concluding thought

The process through which children in psychotherapy start to understand what is going on in and around them in terms of sensations, stressful experiences, feelings that are finding their way, and so on, helps them to question the sense of self of being a 'strange', 'crazy' or 'naughty' child and to transform it. It helps to understand that the 'crazy' thoughts, experiences or behaviours were perhaps the most appropriate responses to strange experiences or situations. Often, one will only be able to find new behaviours or thoughts once one has understood the old ones. In child psychotherapy, we want to scaffold the emergent reflective capacities and narrative competence so as to be able to build on these. In this way, we keep together the bits and pieces of an inner world that is overwhelmed by experiences of meaninglessness, terror, panic, anger and dissociation. Within a therapeutic process, we help a child who has difficulty staying focused and concentrated on activities in which they are engaged in the here and now. We help the child not so much by teaching them new things, but rather by placing a protective dome over a moment when something occurs that initially disrupted the child. Moments in which attention is held for a moment in the here and now, while playing or drawing; moments that contain an opening to another, more meaningful world of experience.

These children (as well as their parents) need words, images and metaphors that are placed like scaffolds around a house under construction and that help them to understand and deal with the 'bizarre' and alienating primitive mechanisms that continue to disrupt their relationship with themselves and others. Scaffolding reflective skills means that a therapist provides thoughts that allow the child and parents to think about things that 'normal parents' of children without trauma do not normally or only exceptionally need to think about. The search for words that tell, explain, connect, and that can be received as meanings that match a child's experience helps these children who have few words available. In an attempt to find new ways to help seriously traumatised children, (1) we search for words that help the child and the parents develop greater awareness of what is going on within a child, (2) we aim to have preliminary notions emerge about how feelings and thoughts work under the surface of relationships and behaviours, (3) we strive for the growth of narrative capacities, and (4) we often see a sense of mastery of one's own behaviour emerge, making the child increasingly less at the mercy of inner forces that drive and direct their behaviour towards fight, flight and freeze modes.

Note

1 Signal anxiety is a warning signal to warn the child that something may be happening so that the child does not recklessly follow their impulses. This signal encourages the child to reflect, to choose a strategy and to evaluate whether the strategy followed leads to the anticipated result, depending on what the environment expects or on what the child thinks is ideal. Signal anxiety therefore serves regulation and integration into the world. In children who have experienced complex trauma, signal anxiety as an important regulatory agent is often lacking or not useful for the child.

7 Islands of trust in an experiential world of unreliable care

DOI: 10.4324/9781003155645–10

Complex trauma is also 'attachment trauma': an inner world built on a basic sense of distrust

For caring parents and other carers who aim to provide children with a warm nest, it is sometimes difficult to understand or accept that a child – following a difficult start in life – will continue to have problems for many years and that benefitting from a good family environment happens only slowly and with great difficulty for some of these children.

In the previous chapters, we wanted to clarify how early childhood trauma can have a deep, lasting influence on future personality development. For example, we have described the insights into (1) how a child's attachment and personality develop as they grow up (Chapter 3), and (2) how regulation problems continually threaten relationships and relational development (Chapter 6). In this chapter, we look at the images of themselves and of others with which these children struggle, and how these relational images are expressed in the environment in which they grow up, as well as in psychotherapy. In psychotherapy, we offer these children a place to express their frightening images and expectations, and we look for opportunities to help them experience 'islands of trust' or 'moments of relational connectedness'. After all, this is a precondition for creating space for warmer and more positive images in their inner world, beside the nasty and frightening ones.

Let us think, going forward, in terms of the 'biopsychosocial trap' (Shalev, 2000), described in the previous chapter: the biologically anchored hyperarousal or excessive pull towards impressions from outside and impulses from within leads to psychological and social difficulties, which in turn cause more anxiety and hyperarousal. A child inevitably tries to protect themselves against this increased arousal and anxiety by manipulating, controlling, rejecting or displaying aggressive behaviour towards the caregiving figures on whom they depend. This largely explains the seemingly unreasonable or senseless behaviour of a child with a traumatic past. However, the child runs the risk of double deprivation: that which took place in the context of their previous life circumstances, and that which finds its source in the child's injured inner world (Boston & Szur, 1983). Because the child perceives the caring and reliable caregiving figures as cruel, cold, insensitive, sadistic, etc., and approaches and treats them from that perception, they also make these relationships difficult in reality. As such, the vicious cycle is – again – complete.

Internal working models: a 'script' for relationships, a map of the social world

In attachment theory, an 'internal working model' (see also Chapter 3) is a blueprint or template that a person has built up within themselves about how relationships work. Such a template works as an expectation pattern about how one will be treated by others: it is a lens through which one looks at relationships. It filters what one hears and sees, where one's attention is drawn to, and how one understands, interprets and gives meaning to these perceptions. As a result, perceptions often confirm what a person previously thought, expected and/or feared. If one expects and fears being abandoned, every experience of the other person turning away, looking away, leaving, of being left alone – even if it's in the hands or the look of a dear grandmother – is seen as proof of that expectation: 'See, you're abandoning me'. Actions by parents meant to educate or set appropriate limits, a message that something is not allowed or not possible, can then be experienced as a lack of care. 'You see, my brother gets a new sweater, and I can't have that T-shirt. Once again, I get nothing'. At such moments, the memory of the new pair of shoes that the child has recently had is very far away. Experiences of 'Once again, I get nothing', 'She's left me alone again' are strung together like beads from a necklace into a more overarching narrative: 'They always abandon me', 'They take better care of others than they do of me' or 'I'm not worth taking good care of', while experiences that don't fit the pattern are not retained as easily or even completely repelled. Due to the powerful effect of these negative images and the tendency not to allow loving and conciliatory images after trauma or injury, past, present and future risk being rigidly blended: the template has already been built on the basis of earlier expectations and filters the perception of new experiences. In this way, it shapes these new experiences. This entails the risk of current and future experiences being coloured by the previous trauma. The trauma of the past overshadows the potential richness of the relationships in the present, and the future possibilities contained within them. The new parental care offered by adoptive parents or foster carers, for example, is not understood by a child with a history of trauma as a new opening, but is interpreted as a repetition of old care experienced as traumatic. In this way, these mechanisms act as a self-fulfilling prophecy. If you are constantly fearful that your parents won't give you anything, and you behave towards them as if that is the case, then you risk – unconsciously and unintentionally – ending up in relationships in which it is effectively more and more difficult for others to give you anything. A parent sometimes sighs and looks away when the child says for the umpteenth time, 'Brother gets another sweater, and I never get anything', or she thinks to herself, 'It doesn't matter if you do something nice for her, she only sees what you haven't done for her'. When, as a caregiving figure, you are treated as though you have negative intentions, or as though you don't like a child, it becomes so difficult to endure that you will inevitably think more often: 'What's the point? Whatever I do, it's never enough'. When parents or caregiving figures really start thinking: 'He should find out what it's actually like to get nothing', and consequently, start acting in line with the child's worst fears (that the child perhaps even unconsciously 'provokes'), a vicious cycle is started, which is hard to break by a family on its own. It is in this way that past negative experiences tend to be repeated. Over time, these templates become a kind of automatic reflex in thinking and experiencing, with a driving force that should not be underestimated. They are as self-evident as water is to a fish. However clear they may be to those who live with this child, these templates are by no means consciously known and controlled by the child themselves. They may once have been true and meaningful, but in later life and in new contexts they often turn simple – sometimes pleasant – family moments or classroom situations into a complex and fraught situation that elicits very difficult affects.

The playroom as a laboratory for social and emotional experiences

Fortunately, this does not mean that existing templates are fixed once and for all, as immovable patterns 'set in stone'. Perhaps they are more comparable to a beaten track through a forest. They show where people have walked previously, and therefore invite the walker to take the same path through the forest in the future, rather than create a new one. It requires countless other experiences to gradually change or redirect this 'beaten track' or 'old foundation', and forge new paths. The existing patterns are so self-evident, the child is barely aware of them. Ladan (2015) therefore refers to these patterns as *vanzelfzwijgende* ('self-silent'): they speak for themselves and direct the child's relational behaviour automatically and implicitly, and so do not present themselves as something that can be discussed. Pointing out these self-silent and unconscious patterns could be compared with trying to point out to a fish that it is water in which it is swimming. In that case, one must be prepared to hear only an indifferent or surprised answer, a kind of 'so what?'. These patterns have a major impact on the life of a child who has experienced complex trauma and on those around them; it is therefore crucial that they learn to perceive and recognise them in themselves, as the basis and condition for not remaining subject to them for life. This recognition of existing patterns can only happen after they have repeated themselves countless times and have caused moments of friction or conflict within a safe family environment. Only then can a child gradually experience that what they think and feel does not correspond to how parents and others in their environment are trying to treat them. Little by little, they will experience that what they do and think spontaneously is not self-evident. Simply drawing someone's attention to these patterns makes little sense, as long as the patterns do not repeat within a meaningful and benevolent relationship. Throwing these patterns at a child in a reproachful or judgemental way is destructive and hinders further growth. You can't blame a child who has experienced complex trauma for these patterns, just as you can't blame someone with poor eyesight for not being able to read what's on the blackboard. What is constructive, both in the short term and in the long term, is offering the child a tool: a benevolent relationship characterised by a reflective attitude from which a child can begin to 'see' their own patterns of engaging in relationships.

First learning to recognise one's own patterns, and then also learning to understand and adjust them afterwards, often requires – in addition to the sustained provision of care by loving parents and a reflective environment – the special context of psychotherapy. Indeed, psychotherapy can be seen as the combination of a special space and a special relationship. The playroom is a demarcated frame 'outside' the child's normal living environment, and the therapist offers a relationship in which they aim to search for these patterns together with the child; what they mean, where they come from, how they currently both reduce anxiety and hinder the child's development and how the child could find alternatives. This combination of a special place and special relationship makes psychotherapy a social and emotional 'laboratory'; a place where the child – often for the first time – dares and can bear to think about what is going on in their inner world, especially when it can be done in a safe environment without immediate consequences for real life. In the continuous stream of small observations that the child therapist makes in the playroom, they try to form a picture of which images and patterns dominate at this time of development, and how they can scaffold the positive images and patterns by placing them under a glass dome that, like a conservatory, can help to make a fragile plant grow, or at least keep it alive. The therapist also looks for ways to contain the negative images and patterns, challenge them and help the child to let go and find a counterweight.

In therapy, Laura plays about 'taking care of someone' for quite a while. At first, she takes care of the therapist; after all, playing the role of the child who is small and dependent is still too difficult. For Laura, the 'taking care of' theme is inextricably linked to intense anxiety about inadequate care: images of witches and baddies suddenly appear, or the play is unexpectedly about pills that make you sick. More positive and caring images only appear some time later, such as a guard offering protection, but the vulnerability of these images is still significant: the guard may suddenly and unexpectedly turn out to be a baddy. Or Laura allows the therapist to play a caring role in the role play, and then soon makes it impossible for the therapist to take good (enough) care of the child protagonist. Laura gradually starts to incorporate more conflicting feelings into her play, such as a child protagonist being angry with the parent. She dares to experiment with these images in the therapy room, but not yet in her real relationships with important caregiving figures.

Bridge testers: the power of and constant struggle with deeply ingrained separation anxiety

When confronted with separation anxiety, children who grow up in good-enough circumstances are invariably comforted by the message that parents will never abandon them. For the fortunate among us, being abandoned is something that occurs in childhood anxieties, nightmares and fairy tales, not in real life. Nonetheless, it is a powerful childhood anxiety that preoccupies every child from time to time. It is no coincidence that the child's experiences of being abandoned, left behind and taken away are common themes in fairy tales and stories, and in children's literature that takes children's inner world seriously. Indeed, this anxiety and its intensity have everything to do with the almost total dependence of young children on caregiving figures. Without caregiving figures and the support they provide, a young child is left all alone to fend for themselves, while they still have a long way to go before having the capability and skills to take care of themselves. As aptly stated by Bettelheim (1976, reprint 1991),

> there is no greater threat in life than that we will be deserted, left all alone. (…) and the younger we are, the more excruciating is our anxiety when we feel deserted, for the young child actually

perishes when not adequately protected or taken care of. Therefore, the ultimate consolidation is that we shall never be deserted.
(p. 145)

But being left behind – even 'just' once in one's life and no matter
how small one was – makes the anxiety of it something that gradually fades or diminishes, but never completely disappears. In children
who grow up and develop quite 'normally' within a safe environment,
this anxiety does not immediately interfere with their general development. In children who have experienced complex trauma, by contrast, the experience of being left behind remains much more intrusive
and real, as something that might reoccur. With these children, this
anxiety cannot simply be 'stored away' in an attic room of their lives,
even with the message from new adoptive parents or foster carers that
they will never leave the child. No matter how sure adoptive parents
and foster carers are that they have chosen with heart and soul to give
this child a place in their home and in their heart, many parents will
have to learn to live with the fact that this will not (completely) reassure the child. No matter how hard and no matter how many times
you say and show in myriad ways that you will always take care of
them, the child wonders why you as a parent would stick around when
the previous parent didn't. So many children who have experienced
complex trauma struggle with deep anxieties of abandonment, which
are triggered by every inevitable separation in day-to-day life. They
attach significance to normal moments of separation, from the deep
conviction that sooner or later these parents or caregiving figures will
also abandon them. This leads to sleeping problems, for example, as
going to bed is part of daily separation moments for every child. For
'normally developing' children, such daily separation moments are
often an exercise in learning to be alone: learning to expect to find the
familiar world the next day as they left it. For children who have experienced complex trauma, however, such moments trigger the deeply
ingrained anxiety of abandonment, that when they wake up – like in
a nightmare or a situation of being found abandoned – everything
familiar has gone. Nightmares about being deserted, being sent to
boarding school, being thrown out, etc. often haunt these children in
their sleep. Children who have experienced complex trauma therefore
test the strength of relational bridges with new caregiving figures for
a long time. When the child has experienced in life that it is not a
given that mums and dads always come back or look for you, they
learn that it is not a good idea to count on someone coming back
each time. If you have ever stood in the middle of a bridge and have

experienced that bridge collapsing under your feet, you will inevitably be overwhelmed by anxiety as soon as you stand in front of or on a bridge again. Maybe you'll do everything you can to avoid that bridge, taking a detour for miles instead, rather than stepping foot on it; or you take a careful step, but are frozen, unable to move a step further; or you'll jump hard at the start of the bridge to test if it can carry the weight and pressure, which nevertheless carries the risk that the bridge will be overloaded and you will make the bridge collapse or break, precisely by having tested it.

Experiencing separation on a small scale

In the playroom, we look for ways to help a child to cautiously start experiencing and believing that small-scale, normal and unavoidable separations and experiences of loss are survivable, that someone who takes care of you also comes back each time. Child psychotherapy offers various opportunities for practising 'separation on a small scale'. Just as going to bed or to school entails a micro moment of separation and being left behind, the separation moments from parents in the waiting room or from the therapist and the playroom at the end of each therapy session also offer such small moments to practise. It is these moments that trigger the anxiety of abandonment, and therefore offer an opportunity to think about and deal with these anxieties in a different way. Doing this together with the therapist and parents helps the child to get to know themselves better, and to practise with these difficult feelings. This often creates initial moments in which the child learns to think about and actually experience that others will come back. They learn – often only gradually and with trial and error – to trust that the parents and the therapist can be a reliable place of refuge and that they can find words and images for the intense anxiety that continues to ambush them from time to time: the anxiety that no one can be trusted. An excerpt from Louise's early phase of treatment illustrates this:

> *Every morning, four-year-old Louise feels lost on the playground after her adoptive mum has dropped her off at school. Her behaviour is more like that of an infant being dropped off at day care. She doesn't seem to be developing any toddler-age*

*skills of bridging this moment of saying goodbye and letting go
of her mum. Only when the teacher takes her to class does she
feel okay again.*

*In the playroom, Louise throws herself to the ground when it's
time to finish playing together with her mum and the therapist. Just
like at home and at school, she can't seem to handle moments of
transition in the playroom. The rhythm of going in and out of the
playroom reminds her of what goes on at school: to and from the
classroom, to and from the playground, etc. – it's all equally difficult. Every loss seems to touch on Louise's 'old' feeling of losing
someone. Who can guarantee that this mum, the teacher or the
therapist will come back? Whereas Louise seems to freeze on the
playground, when she can only rely on herself to find her way back
to the teacher, she gets very angry at the end of the session in the
playroom.*

*The question of how we can help her remember that she is com-
ing back to the therapist next week with her mum results in a game
that will last for many weeks and has different variations. Initially,
the therapist puts one of Louise's favourite play characters on top
of the closet, and at the start of the next session, keeps in mind
that someone is waiting for Louise. Even before the door of the
playroom opens, the therapist wonders aloud 'who is waiting for
Louise behind that door'. In the next phase of the therapy, Louise
actively engages in the play. While standing in front of the door of
the playroom, Louise says, with the same intonation the therapist
used before: 'Who is waiting for Louise now?' After a while, Louise comes up with variations on the theme, sets up other animals,
hides one or other character, and then checks the next session to
see if it is still in the same place. At the same time, she develops
fixed rituals in the playroom that relate to continuity and connectedness. For example, she starts every therapy session in the same
way: listening to the same books on mum's lap. A little while later,
Louise describes an image in which she manages to grasp what her
anxieties are about and what she longs for so desperately. She plays
with a set of Russian matryoshkas, which she takes apart again
and again (disassembles) before putting them back together again
(connects). She says: 'The little one is in mummy's tummy, that
way they can always be together'.*

The witching hour: occasionally overwhelmed by scary, 'witch-like' feelings about others

> *The witching hour, somebody had once whispered to her,*
> *was a special moment in the middle of the night*
> *when every child and every grown-up was in a deep sleep,*
> *and all the dark things came out from hiding*
> *and had the world all to themselves.*
>
> ***Roald Dahl (1982)***

Another metaphor that helps us understand what sometimes goes on in the mind of a child who has experienced complex trauma is that of the 'witching hour', the moment when unexpected and unforeseen dark thoughts suddenly enter the child's mind. Two kinds of experiences in life bring each one of us back to how we experienced the solidity or vulnerability of our first relationships. These are moments of separation and moments of intense stress that activate the attachment system. This means that in the event of an accident, for example – however minor – we usually contact our closest attachment figures first. Their voice, physical proximity or words often bring us the necessary peace of mind to be able to reflect again. In children who have experienced complex trauma, these moments of separation, stress or threat, such as saying goodbye at the school gate, going to camp, staying overnight somewhere else, a parent leaving home for a few days, reactivate the 'old' images of uncaring, unpredictable or absent caregiving figures. The more vulnerable the first relationships with caregiving figures were, the more intense the anxiety and the reactions arising from that anxiety. That is why in children who have experienced complex trauma, these very strong anxieties are sometimes still felt for a long time at moments of stress and separation. Even more surprising for those around them is that even a 'cosy' family situation can evoke anxiety in a child as to whether they really belong there. In other words, what appears to be a nice and pleasant moment may be a moment of stress for a child who has experienced complex trauma, bringing them into a state where the 'witches' 'suddenly' fill their mind.

> *L talks about one afternoon during the holidays when they were working together in the garden at home all day, and picked up fries in the evening. 'Mum's looking at me in that way, I can see she's looking*

at me. The others have fries too, and she doesn't look at them'. When asked what that look means to him, he says: 'She thinks I eat too much, that I cost too much. But she pays for the others'.

Although it was a nice day, and L worked very hard to help get all the work done, clearly enjoying it, at the end of the day he was left with the doubt: 'Do I really belong here? Do I really deserve it?' This anxiety immediately translates into the belief that he is too much or too expensive for the others, and that they begrudge him the fries, and (above all) the cosiness and belongingness.

Regardless of how caring new parents are in reality, children who have experienced complex trauma sometimes – 'suddenly' – experience them as people who fall short, who are tough and unsympathetic, and sometimes even as neglectful and abusive.

The sudden and unexpected nature of how the sequence of rather 'ordinary', simmering, daily experiences is broken is often very upsetting for both the child and those around them: when suddenly something reminds the child of those past experiences or, conversely, when they suddenly realise that they are being treated unusually well and may not have 'deserved it'. In addition to the suddenness, there is also the stalking or haunting nature of these experiences. These are often experiences that haunt a child without them having a grip on them or being able to let go of them – themes and images that stick to them and that continue to haunt them like a shadow from the past. Not only the child, but also those around them need to find a way to deal with images that can unexpectedly interrupt the normal daily flow. Sometimes, a seemingly small reason is enough to turn the interplay that existed between a child who has experienced complex trauma and those around them into counterplay, a scene, a fight. However, the (minor) external cause almost always hides an inner impulse to the outburst or implosion. This negative image overlays the experience and becomes the lens through which the actual experience acquires a negative meaning.

Being able to let positive experiences exist, and to use them to develop positive images about caregiving figures, is an important aspect of the – often difficult – growth process that a child with injuries in their attachment history will face before they can gradually start to feel at home in a caring and warm foster or adoptive family. With a favourable progression, positive, caring, loving and warm images begin to emerge and can exist alongside the negative images. However, the latter only fade away slowly and sometimes flare up again in all ferocity at an unguarded moment, like witches or ghost images. Whereas these ghost images sometimes lead to despair in parents, they are also always a laborious and desperate attempt by the child to bring out and communicate something which they have no idea how to handle internally. The fact that they can express something that haunts them, while having no idea where it comes from, is in itself a hopeful and worthwhile event, as long as there is a context that can contain it. Indeed, it is a question of 'evacuating' images, feelings, and experiences, because they create unbearable stress within the experiential world, hounding and harassing the child. Only in the sufficiently safe environment of a substitute family and/or in psychotherapy can a child gradually start to see these strange shadows as something from which they can create some distance and which they can get a handle on.

Experiencing 'the witching hour' on a small scale

In child psychotherapy, we explicitly make room for children's anxieties and worries. These 'dark thoughts and ghost images' often come from every recess of a child's mind. They almost literally seep into the playroom. It is not uncommon for these children to have images of caregiving figures as witches or zombies; figures who – like the witches in fairy tales and the zombies in films – do not treat children with care but on the contrary, in a destructive and hurtful way.

Celine relates an experience she had at the seaside: 'We saw a footprint, which looked exactly like it was from a bear's paw. My foster mum said we had to be very quiet, and someone else said you should just let them know or hear that you are there'. Celine draws dunes, a path with poles and an electric wire, a puppet. She says: 'If there's a bear standing in front of me, I'm going to whistle a song, and if he doesn't look, I'm going to run or scream, otherwise he'd eat me'.

Drawing and talking about being scared, Celine comes to the scary dreams she sometimes has. 'Once I listened to a song about a bird eating people. Then I dreamt that we were in a garage, and my foster dad wanted to chase a polar bear away from behind the closet. Suddenly, we saw one of my foster dad's eyeballs fall to the ground'. Celine draws her nightmare: she draws her foster dad behind the closet, and – on the left-hand side of the drawing – herself and the other family members who are watching. Suddenly one of her foster dad's eyeballs falls to the ground. 'I often have nightmares', she says, and then talks about a dream she often has, about a zombie.

When Celine is given the opportunity in therapy to express her anxieties, it quickly escalates to threatening images of zombies or bears that want to hurt her. In her experience, caregiving figures like her foster father are full of good intentions to help. In other words, she also has a positive image of a caring person who protects against imminent danger. But that positive image is in danger, it is threatened by ghost and monster images. The positive image can suddenly turn into the image that says 'no one in the world can protect you', not even your foster dad. The positive image doesn't seem to last. In his attempt to protect the others, the foster father loses an eye in the dream.

At the end of the session, after dwelling on the merry-go-round of difficult images, the therapist helps to round up the difficult aspects by providing some time for something that can help Celine become regulated again.

Celine opens a packet of clay and asks for help in softening a ball of clay. While she and the therapist roll a ball of clay through their hands, they reflect for a moment on opening up and closing off so many difficult themes. 'Do you think that when we talk about difficult and scary things, you will be more scared too?' the therapist asks her. 'I do feel a bit scared when I draw and talk about things here, but later at school I won't be scared anymore. Sometimes I feel sad about missing Mum at school. Sometimes I'm sad, and I don't even know why. Then I just say anything at school, for example that I had a fight with my foster mother. I don't want them to think I'm crying for nothing. Sometimes I cry when somebody says: "Just go to your mum to cry a little." Or when the teacher is talking about mums. I miss Dad less, because I see him more often'. Meanwhile, Celine has made a figure out of one of the balls of clay. 'It's an alien', she says. The alien – a creature from another planet – leads to a conversation about 'having gone through a lot', 'feeling different', and about the fact that there's a girl at school whose dad died – a girl who understands Celine. Then she makes a clay 'heart seat bed for the alien'.

The attempt to carry all the difficult feelings like a 'therapeutic container' seems to help Celine. With words, she can express something about how she deals with sadness. In an image, she can express something about how she feels when she feels supported and understood in all her fear and sorrow. She expresses her 'alien feeling', the feeling she shares with many children with a difficult life story: the ever-prevailing feeling of being 'different' from others, the feeling of

Figure 7.1 Celine's heart seat bed for the alien. Photograph by the therapist (Nicole Vliegen).

coming from another planet. But just as much, she shows what it can mean when you can be with that 'different' feeling in a good and warm place in the world. The therapist understands the heart seat bed as a symbol of what her foster family means to her and maybe even her place in therapy. Here, a new image for a new experience is created while talking and playing with clay; like the head of a flower wriggling itself through the earth, a new idea is created that will sit alongside the zombie and ghost images. The image seems to bring an island of peace and positive affect, to a child with an inner world that is often overwhelmed by frightening and destructive images. The image of a heart seat bed also touches on the most essential aspect of being a therapist: being able to provide time and space that function as carriers and containers – or 'heart seat beds' – for the alien themes or ghost images with which many of these children struggle.

Scary on the outside, scared on the inside: rage camouflaging fear

When the fear of unpredictability and disappointment or of being abandoned weighs terribly heavy on the far-too-young shoulders of these children, some of them resolve it by forcefully closing off their fearful inner worlds and retreating into a concrete bunker. They encapsulate these fears and ghosts. With a relationship pattern resembling a hedgehog protecting itself by closing itself off with its spines and keeping others out, these children protect themselves from disappointment and injury, but they also risk ending up in a lonely and secluded place.

Veronica can remain silent at home for hours and even days, often retreating to her room. When her family members try to talk to her, they get a snarl. She resolves a frightening transition to a new school by being very distant and irritable. "You could tell from my posture and face that I was sitting there against my will. I have no need to be social. I'm just waiting to see how it goes. The class left me alone in any case, just as I wanted."

Sometimes children not only encapsulate these heavy feelings of fear and loneliness, but they also envelop their fragile and fearful interior with an angry and heavily armed exterior. An excerpt from Maya's therapy illustrates this phenomenon of shutting themselves off and/or arming themselves and going on the attack.

When Maya is invited to draw what makes her angry, she draws an experience in which she felt abandoned. Then, when she draws what makes her scared, she draws more or less the same thing. The therapist wonders aloud whether it might be that she gets very angry when she is very sad and feels alone inside. Maya looks up, looking the therapist straight in the eye, and says, in a whispered, conspiratorial tone, 'Yes! But no one can know!' Later, the therapist discusses with her whether it is perhaps a good idea that her mum and dad also know, because they will be able to help her better in moments of anger or sadness. When this is discussed later with her parents, dad says that it reminds him of the song Maya loves to listen to. Maya knows straight away what he means and says she will bring it with her next time. Narrative lyrics do mean something to Maya, albeit in a receptive way, through the words of Bart Peeters (translated).

> *If you ever leave me*
> *Then I'll let you go*

> *If there is no way*
> *To talk it over*
> *Then I'll disappear into the cold*
> *& it will all be because of you*
> *Then I'll get drunk every day*
> *& only eat chocolate*
>
> *In subsequent lyrical sections, Maya humorously recognises her*
> *own anger:*
> *I'll lock up my brain*
> *And find any nasty joke funny*
> *I'll vote for zero tolerance and buy a Kalashnikov.*

Hiding to be found: the first cautious sense of trust

Child therapists are often engaged in various forms of playing hide-and-seek. For a beginning therapist, this doesn't always feel very professional: how do you explain to others that you studied for years so you could play hide-and-seek? Like this.

The very earliest game that a child and their caregiving figures play is the game where the child's face disappears under a sheet while they lie on a cushion, and the parent, when the excitement runs high, pulls back the sheet and shouts 'Peek-a-boo!' with a big smile. It is the start of a long time of practising to disappear and reappear in children's play. Hiding objects and yourself, feeling the immense excitement as to whether you will be found, and the equally intense pleasure when the other person finds you. Winnicott (1956) said 'It's a joy to be hidden, but a disaster not to be found' (p. 186). Even Barack Obama understood how important this can be for a young child, when he played hide-and-seek with a young visitor to the White House. Unfortunately, 'hide-and-seek' in Dutch (*verstoppertje* – 'hidey') only refers to one of the actions of this crucial back-and-forth game, whereas the English 'hide-and-seek' refers to the dual aspect of this intense and essential form of child's play. The child doesn't just want to hide, they want to be searched for and found.

A child who has experienced complex trauma often only dares to play hide-and-seek when they can at least dare to count on the other person to actually come looking for them; it takes just enough confidence in the other person to dare to give in to the excitement of this game. That's why playing hide-and-seek in the playroom or in the waiting room of the child therapist is, by definition, a sign of hope. It is almost a daily occurrence in our practice centre for a therapist to look for a child in the waiting room, behind a wall, behind daddy's chair or behind mummy's back. And each time, the therapist and the parents play along. Conversations like the one below are commonplace in the waiting room of our practice centre.

Therapist: 'Where's Alicia now? Didn't she come this time?' Parent: 'No, she's not here this time. She wanted to stay home'. Therapist: 'Oh, what a pity. I was so looking forward to working and playing with her'. Parent: 'Well, I thought I'd come by myself today!' Therapist: 'Yeah, good job you came then. But isn't that a pair of feet there that look just like Alicia's?' Then Alicia comes giggling with excitement and pleasure from behind her mother's back.

By playing hide-and-seek, the child practises endlessly and in a playful way with distance and closeness; with losing sight of, and then finding each other again; with the experience that the other person always comes back and you never disappear from their field of vision forever. As is often the case with hide-and-seek, the control component is crucial: the child initiates the game, sometimes only daring to hide objects for a while, but not yet themselves, or especially wanting the therapist to hide and to see how they will experience and overcome the stress of not being sure that the other person is searching for them. A child who has experienced complex trauma, who is still prone to extreme stress at the idea that they are dependent on the – possibly unpredictable – other person in order to be found, comes out of their hiding place before the other person has a chance to find them or makes the therapist wait a long time before coming to look for them. Sometimes a child dares to run away from the playroom and hides in the toilets, to experience how much effort the therapist will make to keep finding them; or they accuse the therapist – while playing – of being a 'rubbish seeker' who doesn't look for the child well enough, or can't find them fast enough. In this way, elements of a traumatic experience can be therapeutically repeated and possibly mastered in hide-and-seek.

A variation on the theme of this game that recurs in children who have experienced complex trauma is that of falling. Here, too, the English language has a head start in helping to understand exactly what is meant: 'falling and being dropped' (Boston & Szur, 1983) more powerfully sums up how these children are often afraid of 'falling' and of the experience that 'something or someone is dropping you'. In these children's games and nightmares, it is often about the anxiety and despair of falling endlessly into a deep hole, or being left behind somewhere and not being picked up again. This play theme also expresses the hopeful expectation that one will be 'caught' in order to be brought back or to find a way back to the caregiving figures.

More practising with reciprocity and trust in the playroom

In the context of a therapeutic relationship, themes such as those described above are repeatedly played out in order to feel the engagement of the therapist and to gain control over trusting the other and reciprocity in relationships. The more the themes of feeling unsafe can become part of play and communication, the less they traverse and determine real life.

When Dante wants to build a house with the blocks, there is always something missing. The play always gets stuck on something that isn't there: the right size of blocks, the right door, the right colour of roof tiles – it's all the fault of the therapist who 'has so little material'. Carefully and patiently, the therapist – in spite of or because of the large container of blocks – continues to tolerate Dante's assertion that she is lacking something: 'Such a pity that we only have these blocks, Dante! But we're going to have to make do with it!' It takes many sessions before Dante's anger subsides, and he can feel a little more calmly what a pity it is that what he really wants just isn't there. Something can be said cautiously about how difficult it is for him, that feeling of 'lack' that often makes him so angry and at the same time so extremely sad. Only much later does it become possible to also think and talk about how much deprivation there has been in his life, so that every new deprivation is now too much.

When feelings of unsafety, (separation) anxiety, deprivation and threat find their way into the playroom, these experiences can gradually find a place, and the child becomes a little less at their mercy. By therapeutically processing them, anxious and unpleasant thoughts can be tolerated just a little bit better or embedded within other feelings, or partially stopped. Feelings and thoughts are no longer realities that overwhelm or threaten when they are discussed; they are given the status of feelings and thoughts that are allowed to be there as such. This gives the child the feeling of being able to stay in control when these feelings are coming their way, rather than being at the mercy of the waves that are crashing over them.

> *Claudia came for time-limited play-based counselling, during which she 'worked hard' with the images of unsafe and unreliable care she had developed throughout various hospitalisations. The baby doll from the playroom has seen just about every corner of the room, and has had a lot of bad and unreliable food to digest. Claudia likes to come for her 'playtime'. When she has to say good-bye to her therapist, she finds the following play image: with all the large objects she can find in the playroom (table, chairs, mats, etc.), she builds a large obstacle course through the whole room. Then, she asks the therapist to give her a piggy back and carry her through the obstacle course. With this image, Claudia summarises how she was able to show pieces of 'feeling unsafe' and 'having a difficult life' in the playroom – like in an obstacle course – as well as how she felt being carried through it by the therapist.*

Concluding thought

As the loss of a secure base is a dramatic consequence of complex trauma, reconstructing some secure base is essential for recovery (Lieberman & Van Horn, 2004). Being neglected or subjected to violence means an extreme disruption of reciprocity. Instead of reciprocal relationships, there are images of relationships in which one party deprives, dominates, belittles, hurts or treats the other unpredictably. This can lead to a range of 'difficult relationship patterns'. Some children make contact quickly yet in an idealising way, for example: they look for an 'ideal caregiving figure' and seem to find them for a while. The first months in the new home or the initial phase of treatment is then a 'honeymoon' period, with an 'all or nothing' nature to it. That initial idealisation of new caregiving figures can be important for building up regulatory capacities, and consequently, resilience. However, it is not uncommon for minor, ordinary setbacks in the new environment to turn idealisation into a negative, devaluing attitude, and it then takes a while before a certain balance is re-established. Other children have experienced that they are better off on their own than when they engage in relationships. In their expectations, relationships are characterised by struggle and conflict. After a long time in a trust-worthy family and through therapy, they can become attached in a more secure way, but the old foundation of unreliable relationships and the illusion that they'd better fend for themselves remain in the background as a 'last resort'. In the event of a setback, they some-times retreat into themselves – for longer than other children – and it sometimes takes a while before they can mobilise the resilience they have gained in the meantime. Other children show considerable fluc-tuations in the way they connect to others: they sometimes stay out of touch for a while, only to re-establish contact in a very ambivalent way; they may be seeking contact, but in a very controlling way.

The price for the pain from past injuries is often paid by those who remain present in the child's life. This is somewhat comparable to an adult who is the victim of physical pain, showing it and indulging it among those closest to them. In the same way that an adult in pain puts on a brave face to visitors and then becomes exhausted, sad, dis-appointed and angry with their partner, a child can also put on a brave face to the outside world, and take out less charitable feelings on who-ever is closest to them. The cheerful exterior then vanishes as soon as the visitor has left, and the inner inferno becomes fully visible again for a while. Moreover, because these reliable figures are so close, they are inevitably more busy and less available, and then have everything unexpectedly taken out on them.

'First regulate, then relate' was Perry's (2017) advice. The one who will always 'catch' the child when they fall, collapse, stand out or fall into a hole is also the one to whom the child – with all the barbs they have developed along the way – becomes attached. And 'unusually attached' is still attached, although this attachment may also develop some scar tissue!

8 Constructing a story and engaging in relationships as the basis of one's identity

DOI: 10.4324/9781003155645-11

Complex trauma and identity development: in a maze of experiences that are too difficult, one also loses oneself

Feeling that one is alive, knowing what is important to oneself in life, experiencing what makes one tired and from what one draws strength and energy – these are experiences that we are familiar with in our own lives. Entertaining guests during a home-cooked dinner, enjoying a glass of wine and good conversation, being passionate about sports, being able to immerse oneself in drawing and painting, or in a story or a film. It is essentially about vitality and what fills a person with vitality. Children who have experienced complex trauma know little about this fundamentally human experience, as 'trauma compromises the brain area that communicates the physical, embodied feelings of being alive' (van der Kolk, 2014, p. 3). They sometimes barely know who they are, what they find important and what energises them. They have often learnt to adapt to unusual life circumstances and have lost connectedness with themselves as a result of these adaptations, however essential these have been for survival. Their attitude to life is often more reactive: they react mainly to threats (both external and internal) and know less about the experience of thriving in good-enough circumstances and therefore of finding calmness. They are also less able to use such calmness to get to know and develop themselves.

As discussed in previous chapters, growing up in the midst of traumatic circumstances leads to major stress sensitivity and excessive vigilance. The strong focus on potentially unpredictable and negative experiences is often accompanied by feelings of futility ('I am worthless', 'Life doesn't mean much to me') and a lack of vitality and affectivity. One implication of this is that it is difficult to connect with warm and loving feelings, and from there one easily reacts by withdrawing into a detached attitude. Whereas an excess of stressful and negative feelings can be disruptive to a person's regulation, a lack of vital experiences can equally bring a child seriously out of balance. A lack of vitality and the associated feelings of curiosity, interest, enthusiasm, passion, etc. can lead to an oppressive feeling of emptiness and senselessness in some children, on the one hand, and to the experience of lacking an inner compass that helps to shape their life, on the other hand. Such feelings often give rise to thoughts like 'What is the point of life' or 'I might as well not be here'.

In psychotherapy, we look for ways to help a child re-find experiences of vitality ('vitalizing', Alvarez, 1992). This is especially important when the child shows that their existence is characterised by a deep feeling of emptiness and a lack of vitality. Vitality can help to discover who the child is now, how they have become the person they are now, and how they can and want to move on from there.

A numbed inner world: no one knows how long seeds can wait for rain

> **Dead or dormant seeds?**
>
> *Death Valley National Park in the United States is known to be the hottest and driest place in North America. It reaches 57°C in the summer. Death Valley takes its name from the death of the dry, arid earth. Approximately every 10 years Death Valley has a 'super bloom'. In the autumn of 1997, 2004 and 2015, approximately 35ml of water fell onto Death Valley. Millions of seeds then blossom in the spring. The golden carpet of flowers attracts tourists from all over the world. American newspapers and magazines reported on the 2005 Super Bloom:*
>
>> 'No one knows how long seeds can wait for rain. But the last "super bloom" in 2005 led to the blossoming of some flowers that had never been seen before in the park. That indicated that their seeds had been dormant for many years'.

With children whose vitality is threatened, the most priority level of intervention is about giving meaning and significance to early, sometimes barely perceptible experiences. People who work with highly vulnerable children know how they are sometimes barely aware of their own physical sensations and experiences. For example, a child enters the room with a runny nose, or with a pair of trousers that hardly stays on their hips, scarcely seeming to notice. When even basic physical experiences are not really perceived or taken in by the child, let alone consciously gain meaning, there is obviously no psychological space or psychological organisation in which thoughts are thinkable or feelings can be felt.

Such a lack of conscious experience of one's own body (how it is, what goes on in it, the impression it leaves behind) may on the one hand have come about in relationships with poorly mentalizing caregiving figures. The child has had little experience of how small signals, pains, pleasures, etc. can be noticed and can be captured in words and language in order to gain meaning from them. On the other hand, such a lack of connectedness with one's own body can also arise from the 'numbing' mechanisms (van der Kolk, 2014) that play a role in excessive anxiety and sorrow. When feelings are stronger than a person's psychological apparatus can endure, one may try to get rid of or shut out all these powerful and overwhelming feelings, one may try with all one's strength to ignore them by pretending they are not there. This mechanism of 'numbing oneself' can be seen, for example, in how children who have experienced complex trauma, while playing or talking about their play, or about a character, or during a moment of excitement, suddenly let their characters fall asleep, or suddenly break off their play.

However, the problem with shutting down and numbing too many difficult feelings is that it is impossible to close off part of one's feelings in this way without losing connectedness with one's entire emotional world, or at least creating a major imbalance in one's emotional life. You can't just wipe away the dark colours of a painting without damaging the other colours. As soon as you erase a colour, the painting loses its colour palette. Children who handle excessively powerful and negative feelings by ignoring them and 'shutting them down', often end up in a situation where they experience little in the way of affect, and feel 'dead' inside (van der Kolk, 2014, p. 8). Such a lack of vitality in a child who has experienced complex trauma constitutes the deepest level of disruption. Where the connection with one's own deep stream of experience is limited or has become threatened and disturbed, a 'sense of self' (Emde, 1983) can develop more slowly. It is at this level that a therapist begins to work when a child's essential sense of vitality is threatened. In these children, this comes before any other level of therapeutic intervention or processing.

When a child primarily struggles with feelings of lethargy and numbness, and regularly or almost chronically ends up in an apathetic and dissociative state, this is often accompanied by a lack of images of care. In therapy, images of caregiving figures are then strikingly few or even absent. The therapist's task is then to vitalise to some extent the potential seeds of vitality and of caring images – which sometimes appear out of nowhere when these children are playing or talking – and to help the child hold on to these for a while. The therapist searches for signs or flashes of vitality; small experiences in which a child shows some sparkle of positive affect and hope.

Tapping into the source of vitality and placing it under a dome

Petra is rather subdued during the intake interview. She plays in a way that is a bit lethargic and absent. When at the end of the intake she is involved more explicitly and is invited to choose what to play, she chooses a board game to play with her dad. When she is winning, a small smile appears; when she suddenly falls behind during a turn, her mouth gets a bit tense. The therapist asks if she likes to play board games, at which she barely nods and answers in a rather lacklustre tone of voice that she likes to play games. Her father says that she doesn't play games that much at home any more, she prefers to play outside. When the therapist asks what Petra likes to play when she is outside, she answers softly that she likes to ride her bike, and – with a slightly louder voice and more facial expressions – that she also plays hockey. The therapist then asks if she thinks she is good at it. Petra looks at her father and asks very softly: 'Am I good at anything?' Her father puts his hand on her shoulder and responds, 'I wish you could believe that again'.
Vliegen et al. (2016, p. 308)

Due to the intense focus on the themes that bring about some sparkle of positive affect and hope in the child (Muller & Midgley, 2015), a therapist places a protective 'dome' around the sprouting and beginnings of vitality. This is not about artificially 'boosting' a child, but about the therapeutic skill of being alert to and noticing small and almost imperceptible signs of vitality: the sparkle in a glance at a story, the sudden power in a voice at a theme, the unexpected intensity in the motor skills in playing, and so on. Each child often gives small signals of what brings them in touch with a vital flow within themselves. For one child, this is in an activity – such as sports or music – in which they can feel what it is like to want to engage in it, to feel appealed by it or to get a spark of pleasure from it and so on. With another child, you notice that something happens as soon as they feel connected with other people: they start doing something for others; help, cook, take care, etc. Still other children come to life when they can make and create something; when material like clay, paint or paper is passing through their hands, helping them to feel grounded.

Can a child in some way experience something of where talents and desires lie, on an explicit and realistic level, or in terms of wishes, dreams or projects? There is a Japanese word, *ikigai*, which means 'that for which you want to get up in the morning'. For children who, because of a traumatic history, have lost all connectedness with themselves and their inner world, it is essential to find an environment that helps them to experience these sparkles of vitality, to nurture them and to give them a chance to blossom again. They need help more than 'normally developing children' to get involved in activities and plans for the future: they desperately need others to discover what makes life worth living for them, what they think is worth getting up for in the morning.

When a person loses themselves, they lose their inner compass

A child's ability to determine things in life for themselves, to take control of things and to lead them in a particular direction is sometimes referred to in developmental psychology as 'self-agency' (Stern, 1995). This ability originates from a feeling of being a 'self', a person of one's own. In good-enough circumstances, this 'sense of self' emerges in the first weeks and months of life. When the young child grows up in an environment that is characterised by sufficient predictability and calmness, their own core of experience will begin to emerge amidst the diffuse flow of experiences. The child gradually recognises themselves, with their experiences, affects and expectations, against the background of a sufficiently safe, predictable, calm and loving environment. In this environment, the child grows into a more socially active person (a core self): they feel invited and addressed to interact and they feel sufficiently understood, seen and appreciated in their initiatives. The very first 'sense of agency' is then about being able to set something in motion as a child, to get the other person moving by laughing and crying, by pointing at something or by whining. For example, the child can get the other person to pull those silly faces that make them laugh so much, to get the attention and warmth that they love so much or to get that toy that they would like to explore so much. The most interesting 'activity centre' in a young child's life are parents, grandparents and siblings who they can move into pleasant, funny or crazy actions. On the basis of these experiences and of ever-growing perceptual, motor, cognitive, emotional and relational capacities, a child develops: they get to know themselves and their capacities, and develop an 'inner compass'. This 'inner compass' is an image for a feeling of 'This is me, this is what I like, this makes me calm, that makes me happy, that is what I am good at'.

An unpredictable, unsafe and/or unloving environment leads to a completely different foundation of the self-experience. Organisation, coherence and purposefulness either come about too little or are quickly lost again, for example when the child comes under pressure. The child does not experience themselves as part of a meaningful context, they do not get a grip on their own reactions, as a result of which they lose the predictability in themselves and the coherence in their own self-experience. It is difficult for them to focus and maintain a direction or attentional focus. They miss the feeling that they can work from here-and-now experiences and set a course towards a goal.

Ruth Lanius et al. (2004) compared the brain activity of 16 'normal' Canadian adults with that of 18 adults who had suffered from trauma at a young age. Whereas many studies examined brain activity as participants thought back to traumatic experiences, Lanius wanted to find out what happens in our brains when we are not really busy doing anything. While having their brains scanned with an fMRI, these adults were asked to concentrate on their breathing and, as far as possible, not to think about anything and to clear their minds. The study showed that in the 'normal' adults the central structures of the brain were active, starting above the eyes and running through the middle of the brain. These structures play a central role in a 'sense of self'. This was completely different in adults with early negative life experiences. In these people, there was no activity at all in these brain domains involved in a sense of self.

According to van der Kolk (2014, p. 92) there can only be one explanation for this. In dealing with traumatic experiences and the long lingering threat afterwards, the person has learnt to close off the areas of the brain that are responsible for experiencing emotions. This leads, among other things, to a shutting down or underdevelopment of the affective basis of a sense of self. In daily life, the same brain areas are also responsible for registering the entire range of emotions and sensations that form the basis of our self-awareness.

Van der Kolk refers to this as a 'tragic adaptation': in an attempt to shut out frightening feelings, these people lose their capacity to feel fully alive ('deadened'); they have also lost the opportunity to feel connected to themselves and their inner world. This then hampers the capacity to make decisions, because there is no effective 'inner compass' that indicates whether or not a choice 'feels good', or matches with what one really wants to achieve, etc. For example, how can you make choices and make decisions about what you want to study in college if there are no inner feelings that point to whether this is a good choice that suits you? It also limits the feeling of being able to give direction to one's life and to set goals, the feeling of self-agency. The lack of self-awareness can be so great that children who were victims of chronic trauma at a young age do not recognise themselves in the mirror at around 18 months. Brain scans show that this is not merely the result of inattention, but that the structures involved in self-recognition are completely 'out of service'.

Colliding with the world to (re)find one's inner compass

As soon as new opportunities arise in, for example, a foster or an adoptive family, the child tries to resume this self-development. Of course, this does not happen consciously or purposefully: 'Aha, new parents, I'm going to try something new!' Rather, it is a process that follows an important developmental principle: when a child has had a difficult start in life, but subsequently finds calmness and space to discover themselves in better circumstances, they start to try out new emotional and relational possibilities. This developmental mechanism, which we call 'self-righting tendencies', is similar to how a tree grows back towards the light as soon as it gets the chance: the child will try to resume the missed developmental opportunities. At the same time, the old images the child has about themselves and about adult caregiving figures, which are stored by the child based on past experiences and which shape their view of the world and colour new interactions, remain present for a long time. Therefore, this process of 'adapting' to the new environment with new opportunities usually does not take place quietly and gradually, as those around the child would hope or expect, but is often accompanied by a violent inner conflict, with intense emotion and often also with relational struggles.

Without the 'inner compass' that characterises healthy early self-development, the child can only get to know and develop themselves by colliding with the outside world (Winnicott, 1956). The child searches for themselves in reaction to an outside world, rather than finding themselves from a growing organisation of the inner world.

The 'steering' that these children already know is therefore more of a 'steering against' than a steering from within, from an inner compass. These attempts by a child who has experienced complex trauma to find and discover themselves therefore clash with many reactions from the outside world. In other words, what is a desperate attempt to begin to get a sense of oneself in a sufficiently safe environment sometimes ends in a conflict with that environment, reducing the chances of getting this self-development on a healthier developmental track. The people around the child will set limits that are necessary to make living together possible and to help the child feel themselves and their limits. Yet, sometimes the child clashes with the environment to such an extent that they are pushed back, punished or hurt, or that they hurt themselves. What was initially an attempt by an injured and traumatised child to get a grip on or control over their sense of self, then risks resulting in even more loss of control.

It takes these children a while before they can feel what they are feeling in a predictable environment, or dare to realise that they feel very little at all. Moreover, it sometimes takes a lot of 'exaggeration' to start experiencing initial feelings in this new environment. It takes a lot of patience and imagination on the part of the caregiving figures to see why these children exhibit such reactive, clashing and conflict-seeking behaviour. For example, a child will take things away and/or hide things in clumsy attempts to experience that one can have things for oneself, and then deny that they have taken the things in question. With 'normally developing children', we call this behaviour 'stealing' and 'lying'. Through a boundary and/or a sanction, an invitation to make amends, and moral and normative speaking, children are taught that you cannot take things that belong to someone else. However, pedagogical methods like this will have little effect on children who have experienced complex trauma, for quite a while. Indeed, their 'stealing' and 'lying' is a function of their 'remaining in development and motion', and therefore of their psychological survival. As long as they have little awareness of what 'mine' means, they build up little sense of respect for what is 'yours'. This is comparable to how toddlers often cannot and do not want to share their own toys, and sometimes already shout 'Mine!' bringing their precious possessions to safety when someone is just about to look at or touch these toys. However, when at a later age and/or after being repeatedly told off and punished for doing so, a child continues to 'take' or 'hide' things, or is unable to share, such clumsy attempts to get a grip on their life more often lead to negative experiences, punishment or loss of control.

When her foster mother brings Laura to therapy, Laura wants her to tell the therapist what has happened; her foster mother responds that Laura has to 'do her own dirty work'. In the playroom, a conversation about this 'dirty work' can arise, albeit with great distress. It turns out that Laura opened a wrapped gift from her foster father, intended for someone else, to have a look inside. Her foster carers reacted with disappointment and anger to Laura's umpteenth 'violation' of family agreements and rules. With the therapist's help, it is possible to reflect on what thoughts and feelings Laura went through prior to and at the moment she unwrapped the gift, and how she is now especially afraid and sad that it 'will never be okay again' between her and her foster carers.

In a later phase of treatment, Laura says to the therapist on her way to the playroom that she has something to tell her, 'Something very bad that they will have to investigate, and that's what I'm afraid of'. She goes to get drawing material, and while drawing she says that recently she admitted that she 'took' an mp3 player from the sports club, earlier this year. She is able to talk about being afraid – that she doesn't know what will happen to her now – and of feeling ashamed and guilty about her 'theft'. Laura draws a picture in which she expresses her regret to her foster carers about what happened.

Identity development: different chapters in different versions

If a mirror reflects who you are on the outside,
a story reflects who you are on the inside.

Ait Hamou (2015)

Being able to construct an autobiographical life story is an essential aspect of identity development (Wright, 2009). The first ideas of what one's life story looks like originate in early childhood, when the child begins to wonder: 'Where do I come from? Where were you when I didn't exist?' The first brush strokes of this life story, as conceived in the toddler period, are only a first version of a story that builds up, deepens, gains nuances, layer by layer, under the influence of changing cognitive, emotional and relational capacities. Later, questions arise such as: 'Is aunt Lynn Mum's sister? And did you also fight when you were little?' Or 'Where did I get my blue eyes?' and 'Why is uncle Peter never at grandma and grandpa's party?', and so on. The answers a child gets to their questions also grow along with their developmental capacities. This process continues into adulthood, and changes, for example, when parents grow old or die. Children receive information about and understanding of their own life stories, according to their capacities. Actual and imagined elements are linked together to form a coherent story about who one is, affording a sense of stability to one's sense of identity. However, the story is never 'finished'; it is written and rewritten as life goes on, and cognitive and emotional capacities, as well as life events give cause to write the story from a new perspective. The desire to know and understand who you are, how it all began, and how it grew to what it is now, is part of the lifelong process of developing one's identity.

A life story with gaps, leaps and inconsistencies

Complex trauma often goes hand in hand with discontinuities in one's life story. Often, people who have played an important role in one's life story are no longer available or turn out to be unreliable, not only as caregiving figures, but also as sources of information about who one is and what one has been through. In the case of caregiving figures who – for whatever reason – have fallen short, feelings of shame or guilt can interfere with the ability to provide the child with an accurate picture of how difficult it was. Or a disability or psychiatric problem such as psychosis can interfere with the ability to correctly assess the impact that events have on a child's life and development. Precisely because of the gaps or inconsistencies that arise in the child's life story, they are sometimes more intensely absorbed by their life story or, on the contrary, they prefer to stay far away from it. In this regard, Wright (2009) stated 'The adopted person must reckon with the lack of continuity and be able to tolerate this without getting lost in nothingness' (p. 77). The discontinuities in traumatised children's life story and the unavailability of reliable sources of information slow down and prevent them from being able to adapt and adjust their life story flexibly according to their developmental capacities. This can mean that childhood experiences or memories fade away, as they are not kept

alive by pictures and stories. Information can be lost, missed or dis-
torted. Real or imagined experiences or memories are not adjusted
and contextualised, because there is no one in the child's life who has
knowledge of that time. Childlike thoughts about why their parents
gave them up – 'Maybe I was too hard to take care of' or 'Maybe I was
the daughter of a princess and my mum abandoned me because she
wasn't allowed to keep me' – are not gradually adjusted. Questions
about where the scars on their arm are from, whether their dyscalculia
is a family problem and what their little brother's name was, what the
(orphanage) house looked like again, and why it is that they can feel
so terribly hungry, don't find a connection anywhere. Questions about
'That yellow house that keeps coming back in my dream', and if that's
a house they really knew... remain unanswered, nobody can answer
them. The fact that, in cases of inter-country adoption, access to information about a child's genetic baggage is often inaccessible, also
rules out imagining about particular future scenarios: 'Will I grow old
in the same way as my mother?' It also limits the child's ability to consider possible hereditary disorders. Or when you are a foster child due
to a serious psychiatric problem on the part of your biological parents,
it is difficult to make a coherent life story when the parent who once
mistreated or neglected you – because of their own difficulties – now
says that none of this really happened, but that the juvenile court and
the mental health system have conspired to put you in care.

Losing a caregiver entails so much more

In the event of ruptures or discontinuities in life, a (young) child inevitably grieves the loss of the parent(s) and/or caregiving figures who
took care of them during their first days, weeks, months and sometimes even years. Yet, what they lose is about more than just those
trusted and caring people. It's about a complete break with everything
that is self-evident: their world with its rhythms, smells, colours and
sounds suddenly disappears completely. This rupture is comprehensive; few people have to go through such far-reaching events in their
lives. Even when children are adopted at a very young age, they often
have feelings of profound loss and a yearning for elements from the
first period of their life (Brodzinsky et al., 1993).

This early discontinuity in life can be powerfully felt in the child's
being, although the child is unable to find images or words for it; or it
leads to the sense that images and words do not offset the disruptive
feelings that life throws up. For example, the child experiences excessive sensitivity to loss of care, love and approval by others; or a deep

feeling of not belonging; or they do not know how they feel at all but show in severe symptomatic behaviour that they are not okay. Moreover, feelings of loss and abandonment often go hand in hand with an image of oneself as worthless and unworthy of love.

Chris draws himself as a giant rotten egg that stinks so badly that everyone around him is affected by it. The image attests to his deep feeling of being someone who annoys and inconveniences others, of not really being allowed to be there as someone who is liked or is appealing. In the meantime, he goes through life as a boy who makes life difficult for his family, where this image of being someone who gets in the way and is a nuisance is maintained.

Charlotte wonders why her adoptive parents didn't send her back when she turned out to be so difficult, because – so she is convinced – 'Surely you take sour milk back to the supermarket?'

No wonder, then, that feelings of loss, grief and worthlessness are often absorbed in or hidden behind 'difficult behaviour'. After all, it is not easy to dwell on feelings about oneself that are so painful, hurtful and vulnerable. Difficult tensions within oneself are more likely to be communicated indirectly or incomprehensibly, for example in excessively seeking approval, in the endless testing and provoking of caregiving figures, in excessively wanting love and attention or, by contrast, pushing away all love and care; or in symptoms such as depression, or aggression towards others or, by contrast, towards oneself (self-harm). Sometimes, the new caregiving figures are treated so aggressively, increasing the risk of new discontinuities.

Sometimes, vulnerable aspects of autonomy and a sense of self remain relatively unnoticed during the elementary school period. Then, it is only during adolescence or in the transition to young adulthood – when the developmental tasks of developing an identity and finding one's own way in life appeal to a greater extent to autonomy and a sense of self – that it becomes painfully clear how powerful a feeling of being someone worthwhile has been taxed. In order to deal with this unbearable vulnerability, a child sometimes takes decisions that strengthen their sense of autonomy yet disrupt the newly formed relatedness in the new family. After all, a sense of relatedness to others is perceived to be a threat to the fragile sense of self that is more heavily appealed to in adolescence and young adulthood.

Embracing the inevitable scars on one's soul as part of oneself

The most unimaginable discontinuities in life have a disruptive effect on a child. They colour various areas of life and sometimes even jeopardise the essential new caregiving relationships. Experiences that were too overwhelming and/or took place too early for a child to have a clear picture of them are re-enacted in challenging behaviour. They are expressed in symptoms that reveal what is difficult to master.

The therapist searches with the child for images, words or stories that express these experiences. For many children, this has a positive and beneficial effect; for other children, this possibility is no guarantee that early discontinuities can be processed. Nonetheless, finding a translation of experienced stress in images and words is crucial in order to reduce the risk of self-destructive behaviour and to curb dysregulation ('regulate'). For any child who has experienced complex trauma, it is a challenging task to come to terms with the complex life (and the fate at an early age) they have been dealt. As aptly stated by van der Kolk (2014), 'It takes enormous trust and courage to allow yourself to remember' (p. 13). It is about accepting oneself and who one has become, with one's strengths and qualities on the one hand, but also with the vulnerabilities and scars that life has left one with from an early age. An environment that – above and beyond all collisions and conflicts – remains as intact as possible, and does not allow itself to be dragged into the whirlwind of difficulties, is crucial in this regard ('relate'). Furthermore, telling, writing and rewriting one's life story can also have a healing and integrating effect. Weaving together one's personal life experiences – with the gaps and discontinuities, the moments of pain and sorrow, but also of relatedness and happiness – into a personal story can be beneficial. Keeping the various fragments of experience of these children together or connecting them and making them meaningful is very important. Such children express their experiences in dysregulation, in behaviour, or in re-enactments, images, drawings and stories. Keeping these expressions of deeper experiences and forces actively together through containment is also important from the perspective of narrative development. In this context, we regard psychotherapy as creating the space to develop a narrative about oneself and one's personal life history (Pawelczyck, 2012). Having one's own story and daring to own it in the reliable presence of someone else also helps forge one's own identity. By telling the story, the 'autobiographical or narrative self' becomes more coherent and powerful. The narrative or self-story gives structure and coherence to the self-experience.

Concluding thought

In 'normal' development, autobiographical remembering and understanding of oneself lead to a coherent picture of one's personal history (Habermas & Bluck, 2000). As soon as a child develops language, the mode of experience changes in nature. When the environment provides sufficient continuous and predictable care, the verbal and later narrative development brings important new accomplishments. In the preverbal phase, experiences sometimes seem to fade and may suddenly re-emerge as a result of a sensory experience, for example like when the aroma of oatmeal or roses evokes a memory. Yet, from the moment language is acquired, experiences can be captured in words and thus eventually become integrated into one's own life story.

By contrast, in children with early discontinuities in life, the preverbal experiences can be disruptive and overwhelming because they re-activate the old feelings of anxiety, panic or intense confusion. These early negative experiences can be much less easily captured in imagination and narratives, in drawing and telling. Through the active search for images, words and stories, psychotherapy offers building blocks for approaching the trauma of the early discontinuity, making it bearable and giving it meaning in a way that enhances the chances of creativity and healthy development; even though there is the realisation that with this, the traumatic and the destructive cannot be completely undone and will at times still rear its head.

Integrating difficult and conflicting aspects of a human life is a complex task for anyone. It is all the more so for children who have experienced complex trauma. Moreover, what has to be integrated into the autobiographical narrative is of a different – traumatic – order. That basis of early discontinuity in the self-experience requires more language and meaning than is normally the case. At the same time, at stressful moments, language loses its connecting power more quickly. And yet, playing, drawing and talking are and remain central in the further therapeutic trajectory with these children. The challenge for the therapist is to (help) find a language that approximates and can grasp something of the unspeakable discontinuities in these children's early lives – discontinuities that at times are a serious obstacle for them and therefore also for their new families. It is precisely to this end that this book also aims to highlight pathways: continuing to search for images, words and stories in helping these children who have experienced complex trauma, and their families.

> *Can you blame a vase for its fragility or a hand breaking the vase?*
> **Translated from the poem 'Vaas' by Peter Verhelst (2008)**

Epilogue
Ten-point programme for a trauma-sensitive society

> *There can be no keener revelation of a society's soul*
> *than the way in which it treats its children.*
>
> **Nelson Mandela**

With a complex subject like the one covered in this book, arriving at a simple take-home message or checklist is not an easy task. Still, we want to give it a go, and consider how we would summarise our approach as a ten-point programme that aims to contribute to a more trauma-sensitive society.

1. 'They might not remember consciously, but their bodies do!' The tremendous impact of complex trauma on development

In the context of the wide range of developmental domains impacted by complex trauma, these children are primarily affected in their narrative and expressive skills, in their regulatory capacities, in their social and relational competencies and in their sense of self and identity. The narrative and expressive skills have not found the breeding ground for full expansion. The neurobiological ability to cope with stress and unpredictability was tested too early and too heavy to be used flexibly afterwards. The basic sense of trust in others has taken a severe knock. So, there is less tolerance for the frustration of 'normal' day-to-day difficulties and for the 'normal' relational frictions. The child's self-development and personality have adapted to unusual circumstances. In the good-enough circumstances of a later (adoptive or foster) family, the child then suddenly finds themselves in an unusual situation and does not always know how to deal with what – to other people – are ordinary situations.

2. Don't ask 'how disturbed is this child?', ask 'what has this child been through?'

Children who have experienced complex trauma often exhibit behaviour that, at first glance, is not 'logical' or understandable, nor even barely comprehensible. For example, the ferocity with which the child reacts does not match the trigger, or the affect does not fit the situation at all. However, when one understands such behaviour as a trauma response, it is not at all incomprehensible. To panic when one doesn't get something to eat right away; to freak out when one's mother goes to a congress for a few days, even though the child is already 12 years old; to lash out when someone shouts an insult. All this becomes more meaningful taking into account the child's history. Helping such a child to acquire new, more appropriate solutions to life's daily problems doesn't happen by asking: 'Why are you doing that? How disturbed is that!' but by asking questions such as, 'What have you gone through that this situation brings you so out of balance?' and 'What do you need to regain balance?'

Figure 9.1 Three questions to ask oneself in mentalizing traumatised children's behaviour.

3. First aid in case of dysregulation: 'Regulate, then relate, then reason'

Throughout their lives, children suffering from complex trauma have experienced many moments in which stress and affect take over and they lose control over their thinking, feeling and behaviour. Even when these children take steps forward in their development, their parents take into account that there may be temporary steps backwards. The carefully created balance remains less self-evident than with 'normally developing' children. With each new development, an existing (fragile) balance may be put at risk again, and parents may again be confronted with periods of dysregulation. Appealing too quickly to logic and reason never works: 'Why did you destroy your sister's things again?' Indeed, stress and affect have just switched off logic and reason. What these children do need in those moments, however, are parents (or other caregiving figures) who tolerate the fact that dysregulation is inevitable, and who are ready to take over for a while, again and again, comparable to how parents of a child with diabetes or epilepsy are set to take over for a period of time. This is only possible when these caregiving figures are able to keep reflecting, to keep a cool head after countless – and sometimes lifelong – moments of relapse, so as to find out what helps the child to calm down again.

Based on countless moments of regulation, the bond with the child grows. Sometimes only much later, a parent or carer can revisit and talk about what went on: 'Why did you start shouting so angrily back there? What happened inside when you saw that boy looking at you like that?' When the logic and reason button can be switched on again, thinking and talking can become possible again.

4. Remain compassionate to those who provide care

While living with a child who has experienced complex trauma, many sensitive parents have become experts in regulating intense dysregulation and preventing too much conflict. They have often learnt to choose their battles. They sometimes – without realising it themselves – provide the child with a quasi-therapeutic environment. This means, for example, that they do not manage every dysregulation pedagogically, as one would with 'normally developing' children: they do not comment on every negative outburst, they sometimes first endure the violent reactions before discussing them calmly later on ('striking the iron when it's cold(er)'). They tolerate a child staying in their room for hours during a family visit, and occasionally check on them, without obliging the child to be with the family during the visit. In this context, it is hurtful for sensitive parents when those around them confuse cause and effect. Many parents talk about how they are easily perceived – and sometimes even openly addressed – as 'acting weakly in pedagogical terms'. Comments such as 'We would never tolerate such behaviour' are commonplace when a child goes crazy in public. Mental health professionals also sometimes dare to measure parents' pedagogical skills against the behaviour of their traumatised child, attributing the child's dysregulation and behavioural problems to the parents' lack of effective parenting.

5. Listen with care to stories about a lack of care

It becomes really painful when the child's problems are attributed to the new parents' lack of love, care and attention for the child. The negative images about caregiving figures that children who have experienced complex trauma often carry with them also colour their relationships with new caregiving figures. It is not uncommon for these children to remain distrustful of their new caregiving figures for a long time, as they fall prey to feeling deprived and disadvantaged even when being cared for. When a traumatised child complains to neighbours or teachers that 'I didn't get anything from Santa Claus and my sister did', this can authentically reflect something of their internal reality, but not necessarily of the concrete and actual external reality. When a child screams at their parents in public: 'Ouch, you're hurting me!', it can reflect deep anxieties and expectations that adults are going to hurt them, but the child is not necessarily being hurt. Such expressions should therefore be taken seriously as affect or anxiety, without necessarily reflecting the concrete actual reality. As soon as we are reassured that new caregiving figures are 'ordinary', caring parents, they deserve the full confidence that they are actually giving their child what is needed in terms of care, attention, love, trust and material support.

6. The pebble in the pond: trauma affects not only the vulnerable child, but also the people around them

Parents and other people around the child and family often get 'infected' by the stress their child is experiencing. 'Secondary traumatisation' is not inconceivable. When the child's problems come to light, they take up a lot of space within the environment in which a traumatised child is growing up. In this sense, the parents and other children in the family risk the occasional 'toxic shower' and get drawn into situations or behaviour that would not otherwise be part of 'ordinary' family life. For example, they become exhausted and sleep-deprived due to their child's sleeping problems, or they have to protect their child by holding them back when they want to attack another child, or they consent to an admission that neither the child nor the parents would have wanted, or a child who was previously abused shouts at their parents in public that they are hurting them. 'Trauma affects not only those who are directly exposed to it, but also those around them' (van der Kolk, 2014, p. 1).

7. It takes a village…: for some children, new parents aren't enough

Clashing with others, looking for conflict, arguing – as with 'normally developing' children, these are ways to explore one's individuality, and to start feeling who one is. However, the deeper the insecurity about a fundamentally positive and coherent sense of self, the harder it clashes. This collision also has an element of 'checking whether the new environment is solid enough'. The new parents are the preferred target. After all, they are the ones who 'stick around', and one can only take things out on people who stick around. The new parents often have to pay the price for a difficult life with a lot of anxiety, pain and sadness. This means that for some children who have experienced complex trauma, a caregiving network outside the new family is necessary. Particularly in crises that go beyond parents' ability to mentalize and manage them constructively, this proves its worth. A crucial aspect in this regard is that this network of supportive figures and services is on the same wavelength, so that they can support parents and children in searching for a (relative) balance rather than straining the whole system even more.

8. Beware of quick-fix solutions: finding one's way through life with trauma takes time and patience

Complex trauma involves deep wounds in a wide range of developmental domains, often hidden injuries that are tightly covered in order for the person to survive. The child does not allow a new caregiving figure or a therapist to enter into their reality just like that, for fear of being confronted with traumatic experiences again. Comprehensive processing, which will be meaningful to the child's further development, therefore takes time. Supporting a child who has experienced complex trauma in a family and in therapy is a process of trial and error, with many moments of reverting to the 'primeval' sense of distrust. Human time is slow time.

9. Scars: the curse and the blessing

Evolving from injuries in the form of raw open wounds to healed scars is a long road. From a developmental psychological and psychotherapeutic perspective, evolving from raw wounds to healed scars is quite a step forward. From the personal perspective of the child (and those around them), the scars also form a – sometimes lifelong – vulnerability, which can be triggered at a new phase in life or at a new challenge. A new stress factor in life, such as the loss of an important caregiving figure or a loved one, can push hard on that vulnerable spot, and unexpectedly tear the wound open again. Just as the skin loses elasticity when scarring occurs, so the child who has experienced complex trauma develops less flexibly and less sturdily than if the development of basic trust and autonomy had every chance from the start. Yet, it's completely different when a child can live with scars that seal off the rawness and roughness of their wounds: the pain nerves are no longer open and exposed, so they sometimes even forget that they are carrying injuries with them.

10. Nurture every glimmer of hope

'Life's not fair' is a familiar refrain of children and parents in the consultation room. Life for children who have experienced complex trauma, as well as for their parents, sometimes seems like an endless chain of problems: as soon as one has been resolved and dealt with, another one pops up. There are many difficult moments to endure, many bridges to cross, many fires to extinguish and crises to survive. This is where the lives of these children and their parents really do differ from that of the 'average' or 'normally developing' children. The intense anxiety and despair that are part of the lives of both traumatised children and those around them are not of the same order as the minor worries and anxieties that all families contend with.

Every now and then, a bird's eye view is necessary to see the change of course that is taking place in the child's life in the midst of so many difficult moments. Children and parents stick to every little change, quite rightly. 'I didn't panic the very first time at camp, it really helped that Thomas, the camp leader, helped me send a text message to my mum and dad every night that things were okay', or 'For the first time in a long time, yesterday I had a quiet and pleasant conversation with my son, on a terrace at a restaurant. It was nice'. Every glimmer of hope must be nurtured. A good therapist's arsenal includes a cupboard full of glass domes. One for each glimmer of hope. With plenty of sun, water at the right time, and some extra nutrients, a fragile plant can grow.

As every captain knows:
a ship only needs to change course by a few degrees
to arrive in another port.
Adriaan van Dis (Knack, 18 September 2007)

Bibliography and sources of inspiration

Ait Hamou, I. (2015). The dance of storytelling. TED talk. [Video] YouTube. https://www.youtube.com/watch?v=2s7-Ghrzx3E

Allen, J. (2007). Evil, mindblindness, and trauma. *Smith College Studies in Social Work, 77*(1), 9–31.

Allen, J. (2013). *Mentalizing in the development and treatment of attachment trauma.* Barclay.

Allen, J., & Fonagy, P. (2006). *Handbook of mentalization-based treatment.* John Wiley & Sons.

Allen, J., Fonagy, P., & Bateman, A. (2008). *Mentalizing in clinical practice.* American Psychiatric Publishing, Inc.

Alvarez, A. (1992). *Live company. Psychoanalytic psychotherapy with autistic, borderline, deprived and abused children.* Routledge.

Alvarez, A. (2012). *The thinking heart.* Routledge.

Barclay, R. (1995). Autobiographical remembering: Narrative constraints on objectified selves. In D. Rubin (Ed.), *Remembering our past: Studies in autobiographical memory* (pp. 94–125). Cambridge University Press.

Baron-Cohen, S. (1995). *Mindblindness: An essay on autism and theory of mind.* MIT Press.

Benoit, M. (2010). *Human brain mapping.* Wiley.

Bernier, A., & Dozier, M. (2003). Bridging the attachment transmission gap: The role of maternal mind-mindedness. *International Journal of Behavioral Development, 27*(4), 355–365.

Bettelheim, B. (1976 [1991]). *The uses of enchantment. The meaning and importance of fairy tales.* Vintage Books.

Biehal, N. (2014). A sense of belonging. Meanings of family and home in long-term foster care. *British Journal of Social Work, 44*, 955–971.

Bion, W. (1962). A theory of thinking. *International Journal of Psycho-Analysis, 43*(2), 306–310.

Birch, M. (2008). *Finding hope in despair. Clinical studies in infant mental health* (pp. 77–101). Zero to Three.

Bischoff, U. (2016). *Munch.* Taschen Verlag.

Blatt, S. J. (2008). *Polarities of experience: Relatedness and self-definition in personality development, psychopathology, and the therapeutic process.* American Psychological Association.

Blaustein, M., & Kinniburgh, K. (2010). *Treating traumatic stress in children and adolescents: How to foster resilience through attachment, self-regulation and competency.* The Guilford Press.

Bleyen, J. (2012). *Doodgeboren. Een mondelinge geschiedenis van rouw.* De Bezige Bij.

Bonovitz, C. (2004). Unconscious communication and the transmission of loss. *Journal of Infant, Child and Adolescent Psychotherapy, 3*(1), 1–27.

Boston, M., & Szur, R. (Eds.) (1983). *Psychotherapy with severely deprived children.* Routledge & Kegan Paul.

Bowlby, J. (1973). *Separation: Anxiety & anger (Vol II of Attachment and loss).* Hogarth Press.

Bowlby, J. (1979). *The making and breaking of affectional bonds.* Tavistock.

Briggs, A. (Ed.) (2015). *Towards belonging: Negotiating new relationships for adopted children and those in care.* Karnac Books.

Brodzinsky, D. M. (2011). Children's understanding of adoption: Developmental and clinical implications. *Professional Psychology: Research and Practice, 42*(2), 200–207.

Brodzinsky, D. M., Schechter, M. D., & Henig, R. M. (1993). *Being adopted: The lifelong search for self.* Anchor Books.

Casalin, S., Permentier, F., Luyten, P., & Vliegen, N. (2008). The Leuven Adoption Study (LAS): The role of child temperament, parental personality and mentalization in developmental trajectories of adopted children. *Infant Mental Health Journal, 31*(3), 259–260.

Casement, P. J. (2002). *Learning from our mistakes. Beyond dogma in psychoanalysis and psychotherapy.* The Guilford Press.

Christianson, S. Å., & Safer, M. A. (1996). *Emotional events and emotions in autobiographical memories.* Cambridge University Press.

Cicchetti, D., & Beeghly, M. (1987). Symbolic development in maltreated youngsters: An organizational perspective. *New Directions for Child Development, 36,* 47–68.

Cicchetti, D., & Lynch, M. (1995). Failures in the expectable environment and their impact on individual development: The case of child maltreatment. In D. Cicchetti & D. J. Cohen (Eds.), *Developmental psychopathology: Risk, disorder, and adaptation* (Vol. 2, pp. 32–71). John Wiley & Sons.

Cook, A., Blaustein, M., Spinazzola, J., & van der Kolk, B. (2003). *Complex trauma in children and adolescents.* National Child Traumatic Stress Network Complex Trauma Task Force.

Cooper, A., & Redfern, S. (2016). *Reflective parenting. A guide to what's going on in your child's mind.* Routledge.

Dahl, R. (1982). *The big friendly giant.* Jonathan Cape.

De Belie, E., & Van Hove, G. (2004). *Ouderschap onder druk. Ouders en hun kind met een verstandelijke beperking.* Garant.

de Crée, M. (2011). In een bos. In *Barcarolle* (p. 28). Snoeck-Ducaju & Zoon.

Derckx, B. (2011). Somatiek en psyche: Een ondeelbare eenheid. In M. Rexwinkel, M. Schmeets, C. Pannevis, & B. Derckx (Red.), *Handboek infant mental health. Inleiding tot de ouder-kindbehandeling* (pp.46–55). Van Gorcum.

Desmarais, S. (2006). A space to float with someone: Recovering play as a field of repair in work with parents of late-adopted children. *Journal of Child Psychotherapy, 32*(3), 349–364.

de Thierry, B. (2017). *Teaching the child on the trauma continuum.* Jessica Kingsley Publishers.

Edwards, A., Shipman, K., & Brown, A. (2005). The socialization of emotional understanding: A comparison of neglectful and non-neglectful mothers and their children. *Child Maltreatment, 10,* 293–304.

Emde, R. N. (1983). The pre-representational self and its affective core. *The Psychoanalytic Study of the Child, 38*(1), 165–192.

Ensink, K. (2004). *Assessing theory of mind, affective understanding and reflective functioning in primary school age children.* [Doctoral dissertation, University College London]. UCL Discovery. https://discovery.ucl.ac.uk/id/eprint/1446627/

Figley, C. R. (1995). *Compassion fatigue. Coping with secondary traumatic stress disorder in those who treat the traumatized.* Brunner.

Fivush, R., & Hamond, N. R. (1990). Autobiographical memory across the preschool years: Toward reconceptualizing childhood amnesia. In R. Fivush & J. A. Hudson (Eds.), *Emory symposia in cognition, Vol. 3. Knowing and remembering in young children* (pp. 223–248). Cambridge University Press.

Fonagy, P., & Allison, E. (2012). What is mentalization? The concept and its foundations in developmental research. In N. Midgley & I. Vrouva (Eds.), *Minding the child: Mentalization-based interventions with children, young people and their families* (pp. 11–34). Routledge.

Fonagy, P., Gergely, G., Jurist, E., & Target, M. (2002). *Affect regulation, mentalization, and the development of the self.* Other Press.

Fonagy, P., & Target, M. (2002). Psychodynamic approaches to child psychotherapy. In F. Kaslow & J. Magnavita (Eds.), *Comprehensive handbook of psychotherapy, volume 1, psychodynamic/object relations* (pp. 105–132). John Wiley & Sons.

Ford, J., & Courtois, C. A. (2021). Complex PTSD and borderline personality disorder. *Borderline Personality Disorder and Emotion Dysregulation, 8,* 16. doi.org/10.1186/s40479-021-00155-9

Fraiberg, S., Adelson, E., & Shapiro, V. (1975). Ghosts in the nursery. A psychoanalytic approach to the problems of impaired infant-mother relationships. *Journal of the American Academy of Child Psychiatry, 14*(3), 387–421.

Freud, A. (1964 [1967]). Comments on psychic trauma. *The writings of Anna Freud, Vol. 5* (pp. 221–241). International Universities Press.

Gaensburger, T. J. (1995). Trauma in the preverbal period, symptoms, memories and developmental impact. *Psychoanalytic Study of the Child, 50,* 123–149.

Gaskill, R., & Perry, B. (2014). The neurobiological power of play. Using the neurosequential model of therapeutics to guide play in the healing process. In C. Malchiodi & D. Crenshaw (Eds.), *Creative arts and play therapy for attachment problems* (pp.178–194). The Guilford Press.

Gergely, G., & Watson, J. S. (1996). The social biofeedback model of parental affect-mirroring. *The International Journal of Psychoanalysis, 77*(6), 1181–1212.

Gordon, J. S. (2018). *The transformation. Discovering wholeness and healing after trauma.* Harper Collins Publishers.

Göttken, T., & von Klitzing, K. (2018). *Manual for short-term psychoanalytic child psychotherapy (PaCT).* Routledge.

Grünbaum, L. (1997). Psychotherapy with children in refugee families who have survived torture: Containment and understanding of repetitive behavior and play. *Journal of Child Psychotherapy, 23*(3), 437–452.

Grünbaum, L., & Mortensen, K. V. (2018). *Psychodynamic child and adolescent psychotherapy: Theories and methods.* Routledge.

Grünberg, K. & Markert, F. (2016). Child survivors. Geraubte Kindheit. Szenisches Erinnern der Shoah bei Überlebenden, die als Kinder oder Jugendliche Opfer der Nazi-Verfolgung waren. *Psyche, 79*(5), 411–440.

Gruwez, L. (2012). Ronelda S. Kampfer: Santenkraam. *De Standaard,* 7 september 2012.

Gunnar, M. R., & Donzella, B. (2002). Social regulation of the cortisol levels in early human development. *Psychoneuroendocrinology, 27*(1), 199–220.

Gunnar, M., & Quevedo, K. (2007). The neurobiology of stress and development. *Annual Review of Psychology, 58,* 145–173.

Habermas, T., & Bluck, S. (2000). Getting a life: The emergence of the life story in adolescence. *Psychological Bulletin, 126*(5), 748–769.

Haley, D. W., & Stansbury, K. (2003). Infant stress and parent responsiveness: Regulation of physiology and behavior during still-face and reunion. *Child Development, 74*(5), 1534–1546.

Harris, P. (1990). *Children and emotion. The development of psychological understanding.* Blackwell.

Herman, J. L. (1992). Complex PTSD. A syndrome in survivors of prolonged and repeated trauma. *Journal of Traumatic Stress, 5*(3), 377–391.

Hodges, J., & Steele, M. (2000). Effects of abuse on attachment representations: Narrative assessments of abused children. *Journal of Child Psychotherapy, 26*(3), 433–455.

Jenkinson, S. (2001). *The genius of play. Celebrating the spirit of childhood.* Hawthorn Press.

Jongedijk, R. A. (2014). Narrative exposure therapy: An evidence-based treatment for multiple and complex trauma. *European Journal of Psychotraumatology, 5*(1), 26522. https://doi.org/10.3402/ejpt.v5.26522

Kopland, R. (1982). *Dit uitzicht.* Amsterdam: Van Oorschot. (Fragment uit het gedicht 'Verder'.)

Ladan, A. (2015). *Het vanzelfzwijgende. Over psychoanalyse, desillusie en dood.* Boom.

Lanius, R. A., Williamson, P. C., Densmore, M., Boksman, K., Neufeld, R. W., Gati, J. S., & Menon, R. S. (2004). The nature of traumatic memories: A 4-T fMRI functional connectivity analysis. *American Journal of Psychiatry, 161*(1), 36–44.

Lanyado, M. (2017). *Transforming despair to hope. Reflections on psychotherapeutic process with severely neglected and traumatised children.* Routledge.

Lieberman, A., Ippen, C., & Van Horn, P. (2015). *Don't hit my mommy! A manual for child-parent psychotherapy with young children exposed to violence and other trauma.* Zero to Three.

Lieberman, A., & Van Horn, P. (2004). Assessment and treatment of young children exposed to traumatic events. In J. D. Osofsky (Ed.), *Young children and trauma: Intervention and treatment* (pp. 111–138). The Guilford Press.

Lieberman, A., & Van Horn, P. (2005). *Don't hit my mommy! A manual for Child-Parent Psychotherapy with young witnesses of family violence.* Zero to Three.

Lieberman, A., & Van Horn, P. (2011). *Psychotherapy with infants and young children: Repairing the effects of stress and trauma on early attachment.* Zero to Three.

Luyten, P., & Blatt, S. (2013). Interpersonal relatedness and self-definition in normal and disrupted personality development: Retrospect and prospect. *American Psychologist, 68*(3), 172–183.

Luyten, P., Campbell, C., & Fonagy, P. (2020). Borderline personality disorder, complex trauma, and problems with self and identity: A social-communicative approach. *Journal of Personality, 88*(1), 88–105. https://doi.org/10.1111/jopy.12483

Luyten, P., & Fonagy, P. (2019). Mentalizing and trauma. In A. Bateman & P. Fonagy (Eds.) (2019), *Handbook of mentalizing in mental health practice* (2nd ed., pp. 79–99). American Psychiatric Publishing.

Luyten, P., Mayes, L., Fonagy, P., & Nijssens, L. (2017). Parental reflective functioning: Theory, research, and clinical applications. *The Psychoanalytic Study of the Child, 70,* 174–199.

Lyons-Ruth, K., Zeanah, C., & Benoit, D. (2003). Disorder and risk for disorder during infancy and toddlerhood. In E. J. Mash & R. A. Barkley (Eds.), *Child psychopathology* (2nd ed., pp. 589–631). Guilford.

Madigan, S., Atkinson, L., Laurin, K., & Benoit, D. (2012). Attachment and internalizing behavior in early childhood: A meta-analysis. *Developmental Psychology, 49,* 1–18.

Maercker, A. (2021). Development of the new CPTSD diagnosis for ICD-11. *Borderline Personality Disorder and Emotion Dysregulation, 8,* 7. https://doi.org/10.1186/s40479-021-00148-8

Mahler, M., Pine, F., & Bergman, A. (1975). *The psychological birth of the human infant: Symbiosis and individuation.* Basic Books.

Malcorps, S., Vliegen, N., Nijssens, L., Tang, E., Casalin, S., Slade, A., & Luyten, P. (2021). Assessing reflective functioning in prospective adoptive parents. *PLoS ONE, 16*(1):e0245852. https://doi.org/ 10.1371/journal.pone.0245852

Mathelin, C. (2004). What I hear, I can't write. *Journal of Infant, Child and Adolescent Psychotherapy, 3*(3), 369–383.

McLean, S. (2019). *Parenting traumatized children with developmental differences: Strategies to help your child's sensory processing, language development, executive function and challenging behaviours.* Jessica Kingsley Publishers.

Meins, E., Fernyhough, C., Fradley, E., & Tuckey, M. (2001). Rethinking maternal sensitivity: Mothers' comments on infants' mental processes predict security of attachment at 12 months. *Journal of Child Psychology and Psychiatry, 42*(5), 637–648.

Meins, E., Fernyhough, C., Wainwright, R., Clark-Carter, D., Das Cupta, M., Fradley, E., & Tuckey, M. (2003). Pathways to understanding mind: Construct validity and predictive validity of maternal mind-mindedness. *Child Development, 74*(4), 1194–1211.

Meins, E., Fernyhough, C., Wainwright, R., Das Cupta, M., Fradley, E., & Tuckey, M. (2002). Maternal mind-mindedness and attachment security as predictors of theory of mind understanding. *Child Development, 73*(6), 1715–1726.

Midgley, N., & Vrouva, I. (2012). *Minding the child: Mentalization-based interventions with children, young people and their families.* Routledge.

Mortensen, K. V., & Grünbaum, L. (2010). *Play and power.* Routledge.

Muller, N., & Midgley, N. (2015). Approaches to assessment in time-limited Mentalization-Based Therapy for Children (MBT-C). *Frontiers in Psychology, 6,* 1063.

Nadar, K. (2019). *Handbook of trauma, traumatic loss, and adversity in children. Development, adversity's impacts, and methods of intervention.* Routledge.

Naish, S., Dillon, S., & Mitchell, J. (2020). *Therapeutic parenting essentials. Moving from trauma to trust.* Jessica Kingsley Publishers.

Nhat Hanh, T. (1995). *Peace is every step. The path of mindfulness in everyday life.* Ebury Publishing.

Nickman, S. L. (2004). The holding environment in adoption. *Journal of Infant, Child, and Adolescent Psychotherapy, 3*(3), 329–341.

Nickman, S. L., Lewis, R. G., Jellinek, M. S., & Biederman, J. (1994). Adoptive families and professionals: When the experts make things worse. *Journal of the American Academy of Child & Adolescent Psychiatry, 33*(5), 753–755.

Nijssens, L., Vliegen, N., & Luyten, P. (2020). The mediating role of parental reflective functioning in child social-emotional development. *Journal of Child and Family Studies, 29,* 2342–2354. https://doi.org/10.1007/s10826-020-01767-5

Norris, V., & Rodwell, H. (2017). *Parenting with theraplay. Understanding attachment and how to nurture a closer relationship with your child.* Jessica Kingsley Publishers.

Ogden, P., & Fisher, J. (2015). *Sensorimotor psychotherapy. Interventions for trauma and attachment.* Norton & Company.

Ogden, P., & Minton, K. (2000). Sensorimotor psychotherapy: One method for processing traumatic memory. *Traumatology, 6*(3), 149–173.

Ogden, P., Minton, K., & Pain, C. (2006). *Trauma and the body. A sensorimotor approach to psychotherapy.* Norton & Company.

Osofsky, J. D. (Ed.) (2004). *Young children and trauma. Intervention and treat-ment.* The Guilford Press.

Osofsky, J. D. (Ed.) (2011). *Clinical work with traumatized young children.* The Guilford Press.

Papousek, H., & Papousek, M. (1987). A dialectic counterpart to the infant's integrative competence. In J. Osofsky (Ed.), *Handbook of infant develop-ment* (2nd ed., pp. 669–720). John Wiley & Sons.

Pawelczyk, J. (2012). "No stories, no self": Co-constructing personal narra-tives in the psychotherapy session. *Poznań Studies in Contemporary Lin-guistics, 48,* 1–21.

Perry, B. (2001). Childhood experience and the expression of genetic poten-tial: What childhood neglect tells us about nature and nurture. *Brain and Mind, 3,* 79–100.

Perry, B. (2001). The neurodevelopmental impact of violence in childhood. In D. Schetky & E. P. Benedek (Eds.), *Textbook of child and adolescent forensic psychiatry* (pp.221–238). American Psychiatric Press.

Perry, B. (2003). *Effects of traumatic events on children. An introduction.* The Child Trauma Academy.

Perry, B. (2009). Examining child maltreatment through a neurodevelopmen-tal lens: Clinical applications of the neurosequential model of therapeutics. *Journal of Loss and Trauma, 14,* 240–255.

Perry, B. (2017, June). (No. 94) [Audio podcast episode] The Trauma Thera-pist Project. https://www.thetraumatherapistproject.com/podcast/podcast/bruce-perry-md-phd?rq=bruce%20perry

Perry, B., Pollard, R., Blaicley, T., Baker, W., & Vigilante, D. (1995). Child-hood trauma, the neurobiology of adaptation, and 'use-dependent' de-velopment of the brain: How 'states' become 'traits'. *Infant Mental Health Journal, 16*(4), 271–291.

Perry, B., & Szalavitz, M. (2006). *The boy who was raised as a dog, and other stories from a child psychiatrist's notebook.* Basic Books.

Phillips, A. (2010). *On balance.* Penguin Books Ltd.

Piaget, J., & Inhelder, B. (1966). *Le jeu et la naissance de l'intelligence chez l'enfant.* Presses Universitaires de France.

Pivnick, B. (2010). Left without a word: Learning rhythms, rhymes, and reasons in adoption. *Psychoanalytic Inquiry, 30,* 3–24.

Quinton, D., Rushton, A., Dance, C., & Mayes, D. (1998). *Joining new families: A study of adoption and fostering in middle childhood.* John Wiley & Sons.

Roberts, G. (1999). A story of stories. In G. Roberts & J. Holmes (Eds.), *Heal-ing stories: Narrative in psychiatry and psychotherapy* (pp. 3–26). Oxford University Press.

Robinson, F., Luyten, P., & Midgley, N. (2017). Child psychotherapy with looked after and adopted children: A UK national survey of the profession. *Journal of Child Psychotherapy, 43*(2), 258–277. https://doi.org/10.1080/0075417X.2017.1324506

Robinson, F., Luyten, P., & Midgley, N. (2020). The child psychotherapists' role in consultation work with the professional network around looked after children. *Journal of Social Work Practice, 34*(3), 309–324. https://doi.org/10.1080/02650533.2019.1618803

Saint Arnould, D., & Sinha, L. (2019). Hope and fulfillment after complex trauma: Using mixed methods to understand healing. *Frontiers in Psychology, 10*, 2061. https://doi.org/10.3389/fpsyg.2019.02061

Sandler, J. (1967). Trauma, strain and development. In S. Furst (Ed.), *Psychic trauma* (pp.154–174). Basic Books.

Schaefer, C., & Kaduson, H. (2006). *Contemporary play therapy. Theory, research and practice.* The Guilford Press.

Schmeets, M. (2005). Theoretische concepten. In J. E. Verheugt-Pleiter, M. Schmeets, & J. Zevalkink (Red.), *Mentaliseren in de kindertherapie* (pp. 7–20). Koninklijke Van Gorcum.

Schmeets, M. (2011). De neurobiologie van de vroege ontwikkeling. In M. Rexwinkel, M. Schmeets, C. Pannevis, & B. Derckx (Red.), *Handboek infant mental health. Inleiding tot de ouder-kindbehandeling* (pp.33–45). Van Gorcum.

Schore, A. (2009). Attachment trauma and the developing right brain: Origins of pathological dissociation. In P. Dell & J. O'Neil (Eds.), *Dissociation and the dissociative disorders. DSM-V and beyond* (pp. 107–141). Routledge.

Seghers, N. (2013). *Magenta. Werkboek zorg – werk – leven balans voor ouders van een zorgenkind.* KU Leuven.

Sells, S. P., & Souder, E. (2017). *Treating the traumatized child. A step-by-step family systems approach.* Springer.

Shalev, A. Y. (2000). Post-traumatic stress disorder: Diagnosis, history and life course. In D. Nutt, J. R. T. Davidson, & J. Zohar (Eds.), *Post-traumatic stress disorder: Diagnosis, management and treatment* (pp. 1–15). Martin Dunitz.

Sharp, C., & Fonagy, P. (2008). The parent's capacity to treat the child as a psychological agent: Constructs, measures and implications for developmental psychopathology. *Social Development, 17*(3), 737–754.

Shipman, K., & Zeman, J. (2001). Socialization of children's emotion regulation in mother-child dyads: A developmental psychopathology perspective. *Development and Psychopathology, 13*(2), 317–336.

Slade, A. (1994). Making meaning and making believe: Their role in the clinical process. In A. Slade & D. Wolf (Eds.), *Children at play. Clinical and developmental approaches to meaning and representation* (pp. 81–107). Oxford University Press.

Slade, A., Grienenberger, J., Bernbach, E., Levy, D., & Locker, A. (2005). Maternal reflective functioning, attachment, and the transmission gap: A preliminary study. *Attachment & Human Development, 7*(3), 283–298.

Solomon, E. P., & Heide, K. M. (1999). Type III trauma: Toward a more effective conceptualization of psychological trauma. *International Journal of Offender Therapy and Comparative Criminology, 43*(1), 202–210.

Solms, M. L. (2018). The neurobiological underpinnings of psychoanalytic theory and therapy. *Frontiers of Behavioral Neurosciences, 12*, 294. https://doi.org/10.3389/fnbeh.2018.00294

Spitz, R. A. (1965). *The first year of life. A psychoanalytic study of normal and deviant developmental object relations.* International Universities Press.

Steele, M., Hodges, J., Kaniuk, J., Hillman, S., & Henderson, K. (2003). Attachment representations and adoption: Associations between maternal states of mind and emotion narratives in previously maltreated children. *Journal of Child Psychotherapy, 29*(2), 187–205.

Steele, M., Hodges, J., Kaniuk, J., & Steele, H. (2010). Mental representation and change: Developing attachment relationships in an adoption context. *Psychoanalytic Inquiry, 30,* 25–40.

Stern, D. N. (1985). *The interpersonal world of the infant.* Karnac.

Stern, D. N. (1989). Developmental prerequisites for the sense of narrated self. In A. M. Cooper, O. F. Kernberg, & E. S. Person (Eds.) (1989), *Psychoanalysis: Toward the second century* (pp. 168–178). Yale University Press.

Stern, D. N. (1995). The parent-infant interaction. In *The motherhood constellation. A unified view of parent-infant psychotherapy* (pp. 59–78). Basic Books.

Struik, A. (2010). *Slapende honden? Wakker maken! Een stabilisatiemethode voor chronisch getraumatiseerde kinderen.* Pearson Assessment and Information.

Struik, A. (2016). *Treating chronically traumatized children: Don't let sleeping dogs lie!* (2nd ed.) Routledge.

Szalavitz, M., & Perry, B. (2010). In your face. In *Born for love. When empathy is essential and endangered* (pp. 27–44). Harper Collins Publishers.

Tang, E., Bleys, D., & Vliegen, N. (2018). Making sense of adopted children's internal reality using Narrative Story Stem Techniques: A mixed-methods synthesis. *Frontiers in Psychology, 9,* 1189. https://doi.org/10.3389/fpsyg.2018.01189.

Terr, L. C. (1991). Childhood traumas: An outline and overview. *American Journal of Psychiatry, 148*(1), 10–20. https://doi.org/ 10.1176/ajp.148.1.10

Terr, L. C (2008). *Too scared to cry: Psychic trauma in childhood.* Basic Books.

Tronick, E., Adamson, L. B., Als, H., & Brazelton, T. B. (1975, April). Infant emotions in normal and perturbated interactions. In *Biennial meeting of the society for research in child development,* Denver, CO.

Tronick, E. Z., & Gianino, A. (1986). Interactive mismatch and repair: Challenges to the coping infant. *Zero to Three, 6*(3), 1–6.

Tuber, S. (2012). The clinical implications of aspects of a child's degree of psychological mindedness in dynamically oriented child psychotherapy. *Journal of Infant, Child and Adolescent Psychotherapy, 11,* 3–20.

Turnbull, G. (2012). *Gevangen in je hoofd. Hoe verwerkt ons brein een trauma.* A.W. Bruna Uitgevers.

van der Kolk, B. (2014). *The body keeps the score. Brain, mind, and body in the healing of trauma.* The Penguin Group.

van der Kolk, B. A. (1996). The complexity of adaptation to trauma: Self-regulation, stimulus discrimination, and characterological development. In B. A. van der Kolk, A. C. McFarlane, & L. Weisaeth (Eds.), *Traumatic stress: The effects of overwhelming experience on mind, body, and society* (pp. 182–213). The Guilford Press.

van der Kolk, B. A. (2003). The neurobiology of childhood trauma and abuse. *Child and Adolescent Psychiatric Clinics of North America, 12*(2), 293–317.

van der Kolk, B. A. (2005). Developmental trauma disorder: Toward a rational diagnosis for children with complex trauma histories. *Psychiatric Annals, 35*(5), 401–408.

van der Kolk, B. A., Pynoos, R. S., Cicchetti, D., Cloitre, M., D'Andrea, W., Ford, J. D., Lieberman, A. F., Putnam, F. W., Saxe, G., Spinazzola, J., Stolbach, B. C., & Teicher, M. (2009). *Proposal to include a developmental trauma disorder diagnosis for children and adolescents in DSM-V.* Complex Trauma Treatment Network. https://www.cttntraumatraining.org/uploads/4/6/2/3/46231093/dsm-v_proposal-dtd_taskforce.pdf

van Dis, A. (2007). Interview in *Knack*, 18 September 2007.

van Egmond, G. (1987). *Bodemloos bestaan. Het Geen-Bodem-Syndroom, problemen met adoptiekinderen.* Ambo.

Van Horn, P. (2011). The impact of trauma on the developing social brain: Development and regulation in relationship. In J. D. Osofsky (Ed.), *Clinical work with traumatized young children* (pp. 11–30). The Guilford Press.

Verhelst, P. (2008). *Sterrebeelden.* Prometheus.

Verheugt-Pleiter, A., Zevalkink, J., & Schmeets, M. (2008). *Mentalizing in child therapy. Guidelines for clinical practitioners.* Karnac.

Vliegen, N. (2006). *Kleine baby's, prille ouders. Samen in ontwikkeling.* Acco.

Vliegen, N., Hannes, K., & Meurs, P. (2016). De complexiteit van klinische psychodiagnostiek vraagt methodologische diversiteit. *Tijdschrift Klinische Psychologie, 46*(4), 302–316.

Vliegen, N., Tang, E., Midgley, N., Luyten, P., & Fonagy, P. (in press). *Therapeutic work for children with complex trauma: A three-track psychodynamic approach.* Routledge.

Willock, B. (1986). Narcissistic vulnerability in the hyperaggressive child: The disregarded (unloved, uncared-for) self. *Psychoanalytic Psychology, 3*(1), 59–80. https://doi.org/10.1037/0736-9735.3.1.59

Winnicott, D. W. W. (1956). The antisocial tendency. In D. W. W. Winnicott (1984), *Deprivation and delinquency* (pp. 103–112). Tavistock Publications.

Winnicott, D. W. W. (1965). *The maturational processes and the facilitating environment: Studies in the theory of emotional development.* The Hogarth Press and the Institute of Psycho-Analysis.

Winnicott, D. W. W. (1971). *Playing and reality.* Routledge.

Wright, J. (2009). The princess has to die. Representing rupture and grief in the narrative of adoption. *Psychoanalytic Study of the Child, 64,* 75–91.

Yanof, J. A. (2019). Play in the analytic setting: The development and communication of meaning in child analysis. *The International Journal of Psychoanalysis, 100*(6), 1390–1404. https://doi.org/10.1080/00207578.2019.1642758

Zeman, J., Shipman, K., & Suveg, C. (2002). Anger and sadness regulation: Predictions to internalizing and externalizing symptoms in children. *Journal of Clinical Child & Adolescent Psychology, 31*(3), 393–398.

Index

Note: **Bold** page numbers refer to tables; *italic* page numbers refer to figures and page numbers followed by "n" denote endnotes.

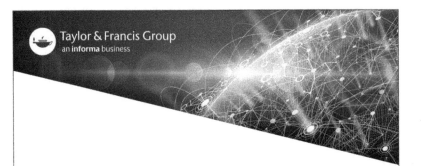